CONSTANTINOPLE

ICONOGRAPHY OF A SACRED CITY

PHILIP SHERRARD

LONDON
OXFORD UNIVERSITY PRESS
NEW YORK · TORONTO
1965

Oxford University Press, Amen House, London E.C. 4

GLASGOW NEW YORK TORONTO MELBOURNE WELLINGTON BOMBAY CALCUTTA MADRAS
KARACHI KUALA LUMPUR CAPE TOWN IBADAN NAIROBI ACCRA

PRINTED IN SWITZERLAND

CONSTANTINOPLE
ICONOGRAPHY OF A SACRED CITY

TO ZISIMOS LORENZATOS

CONTENTS

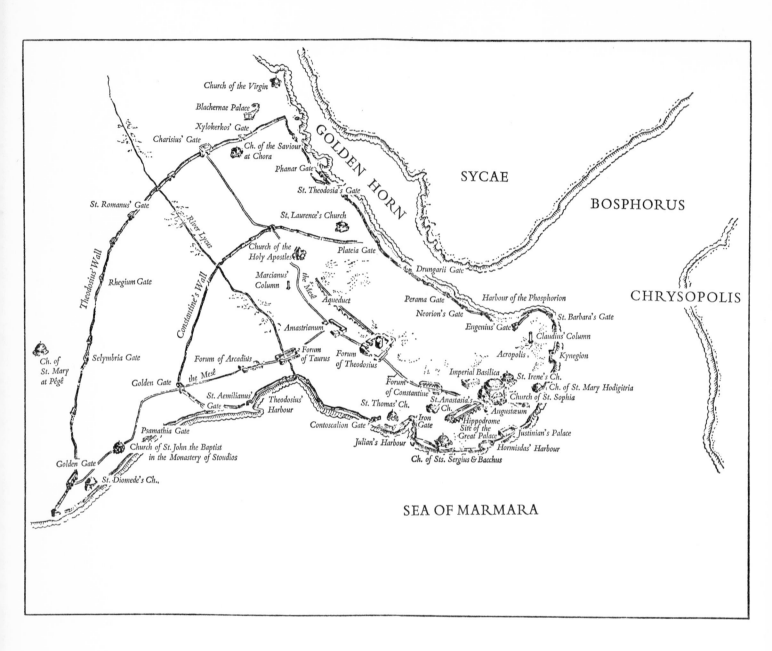

Plan of Constantinople in the time of Justinian, after Glanville Downey.

Place, People, and Buildings

When after the defeat of Licinius in A.D. 323 Constantine, now sole surviving Caesar of the Roman Empire, found himself faced with the task of arresting the disintegration of his inheritance and of welding its heterogeneous elements, territorial and cultural, into a new coherence, one of his first concerns was with the choice and construction of a new imperial capital. Where should he place this? Rome was the scene of conspiracy and intrigue; north and west lay lands of unreclaimed barbarity. The east seemed the obvious choice. It was in the east that some bulwark had to be found to resist the Parthians and to check the westerly migrations from the Steppes; it was the main focus of trade; and it was there that Christianity was rapidly gaining an ascendancy sufficient for it to replace the dead or dying religions of the ancient world. But if in the east, then where? Nicodemia might well have served had it not been associated too vividly with the persecutions of Diocletian for it to find favour with an Emperor whose policy and patronage were directed more and more towards the protection of the Christians. Chalcedon, on the Bosphorus, was a second possibility; but, as Polybius had pointed out several centuries before, winds and currents made it difficult to reach by sea, the main means of access; and in any case, as later hagiography reveals, when Constantine did in fact think of settling his city there, supernatural augury delivered through the flight of eagles made it clear that it was not on this spot that the divine will had determined to build the 'city of the Mother of God'; on the contrary, it was to be built on the opposite shore, there where, some thousand years before, Byzas, son of Neptune, had founded the small town that still, down to Constantine's day, bore his name and some of whose natural advantages Constantine had already experienced in his wars against his late rival for the throne.

Indeed, what better site than this could have been found? Set on a triangular peninsula at the junction of many waters, sweet and salt, Byzantium seemed to fulfil all the standards of beauty, security, and commercial viability that the most demanding founder of cities could require. Northwards a narrow channel, the Bosphorus, linking the Propontis or Sea of Marmara to the Black Sea, wound for some seventeen miles between a double range of hills whose downland or rocky outcrops broke through a mixed assemblage of scrub and tree—dwarf oaks, junipers, giant heath, bracken, broom, bay-trees, the occasional pine. Streams fulfilled their journeys through groves of bamboo at the mouths of grassy valleys, the scent of flowers made soft the air. Here too the terror and devotion of seamen heading, as once the Argonauts, for the Black Sea, had planted votive shrines, temples. Obscene harpies chirped in a deserted palace. Where the Bosphorus terminated stood the Cyanian rocks, screening from the eye of profane curiosity the waters of the Black Sea. Through the ports of this sea from the enormous Russia beyond were later to flow corn and furs, caviare and salt, honey and gold, wax and slaves for sale in the markets of the imperial capital. To the south, beyond the Sea of Marmara, beyond a second strait, the Hellespont, by whose narrow channel the kiss of Europe and Asia is again frustrated, lay the Aegean and the rich gardens of Asia Minor, with the flax fields and granaries of Egypt behind them. To the east, as far as India and China, stretched the trade-routes along which were to pass those treasured spices and medicaments—pepper and musk, cloves and nutmeg, cinnamon and camphor, sugar and ginger, aloes and balsam—which were to lend such refinement to the Byzantine cuisine, as well as the ivory and amber, pearls and precious stones, porcelain and glass, muslin, taffeta, and damask which were to form some of the basic raw materials of such exquisite products of Byzantine craftsmanship as the reliquaries and embroideries. Westwards, where Byzantium's triangular peninsula joined the European mass, stretched a rich prospect of vineyards, gardens, and fields of corn. Fish teemed in the waters of the Marmara and Bosphorus. And almost where these waters met and merged another creek led off along the northern shore of the city's triangle to form a perfect natural harbour, the Golden Horn, whose bay did indeed curve like a stag's antler or the horn of an ox to meet at its western tip the fresh waters of incoming streams. And this bay, as the sixth-century Byzantine writer, Procopius, was to observe, *is always calm, being made by nature never to be stormy, as though limits were set to the billows and the surge was shut out in the city's honour. And in winter when harsh winds fall upon the sea and the strait (the Bosphorus), as soon as ships reach the bay's entrance, they can proceed without pilot and moor easily. The whole bay is above forty stades round, and all of it is a harbour, so that when a ship anchors there the stern rides on the sea while the prow rests on land, as if the two elements rivalled each other in their desire to be of greatest service to the city.*[1]

Here then, on this sea-girt promontory, Constantine was to build his city. Of the pre-Constantinian city, confined as it was within the wall which, running from the Golden Horn to the Sea of Marmara, enclosed but the final hill of the peninsula, there remained what had partially been rebuilt by the Emperor Septimius Severus after he had destroyed the town in A.D. 196: the Tetrastoon or Place of the Four Porticos; the incomplete Hippodrome; the Bath of Zeuxippus. Ignoring the ancient boundaries, Constantine, lance in hand, himself assumed the task of marking out the area within which he proposed to erect his new capital. As he advanced westwards, including first a second hill, then a third, and so on, until, on the model of the old Rome, seven hills were embraced within the area, consternation and alarm at the improbable magnitude of the site, which already exceeded that of the most ample city, overcame his assistants. 'Whither, Master, are you going?' Constantine was asked. To which he replied: 'I shall advance to where he who goes before me stops.'[2] In A.D. 325 the site was consecrated and the building began. Material was at hand in the marbles of the Proconnesus, a group of islands in the Sea of Marmara, and in the wood from forests bordering the Black Sea. Of these, edifice after edifice rose upon the consecrated ground. Streets were laid, *fora* and gardens, churches and palaces, gates and porticos succeeded one another with a bewildering rapidity and profusion. To adorn his city Constantine looted the artistic treasures of the whole Greco-Roman world—*pene omnium urbium nuditate.* The Artemision at Ephesus; the Athenaion at Lindos in Rhodes; the temple of Zeus at Dodona; Castor and Pollux; the Delphic Apollo; the Muses of Helicon; the Cyzicene Rhea; the Genius of Rome; the four horses of Lysippus (further displaced to the façade of the church of San Marco at Venice where, after an interlude on the Arc de Triomphe, they still survive); bronze eagle and Calydonian boar; the bronze triple pillar from Delphi on which were written the names of the thirty-one Greek states that took part in the victory at Plataea over the armies of the Persian Xerxes in 479 B.C.: these were some of the sanctuaries and some of the works on which Constantine drew for the decoration of his new capital. Christian emblems occupied some of the more prominent positions: before the entrance to the imperial palace Constantine placed an encaustic painting of himself, his head surmounted by a cross, surrounded by his children, while a serpent, signifying the enemies of the cross, plunged into an abyss at their feet; and three monumental crosses kept guard over three of the city's main areas.

On 11 May 330, the city was dedicated. The dedicatory procession, presided over by a priest and accompanying the statue-reliquary of Constantine Helios—a bronze Apollo whose head had been replaced by that of the Emperor encircled by the golden rays of the sun, the rays being no less than the nails that had pierced Christ on the Cross—this procession started out at a westerly point in the city known as Philadelphion. Followed by white-clad senators and the chief imperial dignitaries, white candles fluttering in their hands, the cortège made its way towards the great forum named after the founder himself, the Forum of Constantine. There, at the foot of a huge column whose eight drums of porphyry, bound in metal, stood on a white marble plinth, the statue was deposited. At the base of the column were buried

8

the sacred trophies of that double tradition, Christian and Roman, the spirit of Jerusalem and the spirit of Rome, which was to determine the course of the city's history down to its final day: relics of saints; crumbs from the bread with which Christ had fed the five thousand in the wilderness; the crosses of the two thieves crucified with Christ which the Emperor's mother, St. Helena of York, had recently brought from Jerusalem; the alabaster box of ointment of spikenard; the adze with which Noah built the ark; the rock from which water sprang when touched by the rod of Moses; and finally the Palladium which Aeneas had taken from Troy to Italy and which had now been brought to Constantine's city to signify the establishment of Roman *fortuna* on the banks of the Bosphorus. By means of a special contraption set up for the purpose and to the accompaniment of the interminable chant of 'Kyrie eleison', the statue-reliquary (for it also enclosed a fragment from Christ's Cross) was hoisted into its position at the top of the column, some 117 feet above the ground. When the litany ceased, the priest proclaimed the name of the new imperial capital: *Constantinopolis*, the city of Constantine. 'Then the city that was called Constantine was saluted with acclamations, while all the priests cried aloud: "O Lord, guide it on the good path for infinite ages."' Constantine Helios, aloft on his shaft of reddish-purple Egyptian stone, bore in his right hand a sceptre (or, as another chronicler would have it, a lance), and in his left hand a globe, image of the world, on which stood a winged victory, later to be replaced by a cross. The inscription ran: 'O Christ, Ruler and Master of the World, to You now I dedicate this subject City, and these Sceptres, and the Might of Rome. Protector, save her from all harm.'

The next day there were games in the Hippodrome and other rites, less Christian in character. *Now he (Constantine) had had another statue of himself made, in sculptured wood, all gilded, carrying in the right hand the Tychê of the city, this gilded also. He ordered that on the day on which the games were given in honour of the dies natalis of the city, soldiers..., holding a white candle in the hand, should escort this wooden statue and that the chariot which bore it* (referred to as the Chariot of the Sun), *after having circled the upper* camptos *of the Hippodrome, should be placed in front of the imperial box. The same ceremony should be repeated in future on each anniversary, and the reigning Emperor should rise from his throne and should adore the statue of the Emperor Constantine and of the Tychê of the city... Thus, amid an innumerable throng of people, the festival continued for forty days, accompanied by the frequent distributions of largess on the part of the Emperor to the populace. At the end of this period, each retired to his own dwelling-place.*

*

The disposition of the city that Constantine built and to which he gave his name was to remain unchanged in all its main features throughout the Byzantine period. The actual area of the Constantinian city, large though it had at first seemed, soon, under the pressure of a growing populace, proved inadequate, and was enlarged to include another slice of terrain between the Golden Horn and the Propontis; and it was to the west of this extended area that in 439 Cyrus, prefect of the city under the Emperor Theodosius II, built a huge triple line of walls across the five-mile landward base of the promontory in order to defend the new suburbs. This line of walls, the impressive ruins of which can still be seen today, marked from then on the western limit of the city. But perhaps the greatest change in the actual physical appearance of the city took place when, after the Nika Rebellion in 532 and the accompanying fire which burnt half the original city to the ground, the Emperor Justinian (527–565) began that great spate of building which, to the excessive strain of the imperial treasury, was so to dazzle his own and subsequent generations. Everywhere arose, as though conjured forth by some insatiable supernatural agency, palaces, churches, baths, aqueducts, great cisterns supported on exquisitely carved columns, new markets, houses for great nobles, barracks, hospitals, convents. The magnificence of the new city, its richness of

Illustration opposite: Marble portrait-head of a Byzantine dignitary of the fourth century from Aphrodisias. Musées du Cinquantenaire, Brussels. Copyright A.C.L. Brussels.

decoration, marbles, statuary, mosaics, struck all with amazement. Chroniclers, usually concerned only with military exploits and court intrigue, interrupt their narratives to speak of measurements and designs, architects and artefacts, to collect lists of gems, to number the marvels of decoration. *O what a splendid city*, a later visitor[3] from the West was to exclaim, *how stately, how fair, how many monasteries therein, how many palaces raised by sheer labour in its broadways and streets, how many works of art, marvellous to behold: it would be wearisome to tell of the abundance of all good things; of gold and of silver, garments of manifold fashion and such sacred relics. Ships are at all times putting in at this port, so that there is nothing that men want that is not brought hither.*

Indeed, had one, at one of the brilliant periods of the city's history, at some time, say, during the reigns of the great Macedonian Emperors, between the years 867 and 1057, or of the Comneni in the latter half of the eleventh century, sailed down the Bosphorus, where, in the gulfs formed by its folds, the luxury yachts of the Byzantine nobility and the rich merchants, painted vermilion or gold, swung at anchor and where, near falling streams, on moles prolonged into the sea, the golden roofs of the summer palaces glittered among cypresses and vines; and had one then entered the port of the Golden Horn, one would have been confronted by a rare and startling array of boats: barks of Dalmatians or Croats; the *monoxyla* of the Russians; *caïques* of antique type from the Greek islands, their prows pouting like a swan's breast; the high galleys of Genoa, Venice, or Amalfi; light *feluccas* from the east; the long *chelandia* of the imperial Byzantine fleet, equipped with *ballista* and tubes, ending in the bronze throat of a lion, for the discharge of fire. Passing into the city through one of the gates opening on to the shores of the Golden Horn, one would have found oneself in a forest of streets narrow or broad, squalid or majestic, winding hither and thither between rows of houses, mostly wooden and two storeys high, and supporting wooden balconies, though those of the wealthier citizens would be of long narrow bricks faced with cut stone or marble and built round a central court with a fountain and an ornamental garden. The main streets, such as that known as the Mesê, or Middle Street, the central highway of the city whose chief arm ran from the great Golden Gate in the south-west corner of Theodosius' wall to close to the entrance of the Imperial Palace, would be bordered by columned porticos, interrupted by monumental squares, dominated by the domes of churches 'more numerous than days in the year', by high columns bearing aloft the statues of Emperor and Empress. Along this street, the Mesê, in particular stretched the bazaars of the city: here were piled the products of Byzantium's luxury industries; here too, beneath the porticos and in the squares, the various trade-guilds of the city had their quarters: jewellers, furriers, wax-chandlers, bakers, merchants of silk and linen, pork-butchers and fishmongers, until, at the gate to the Great Palace itself, beneath the icon of Christ that now (replacing Constantine's emblem) stood above its brazen door, the perfumers had their stalls, 'so that the sweet perfume may waft upwards to the icon and at the same time permeate the vestibule of the Imperial Palace'.[4] Such a courtship of the senses would be debased by the name of aestheticism, for it was never separated from religious context or practical service; but everywhere its effects were visible: in the carved statues, painted walls, corbels, and screens of church, palace, guild-hall, or burgher's house; in the goods displayed to the gaze of all on market stalls, in the silks and brocades, copper and cool gold, tooled leather and brilliant glass, reliquary and earring, brooch and chalice; in the fruits and vegetables set out in their panniers under the open sky.

Everywhere too, in the vaulted bazaars, in the sun-drenched squares, beneath towers round, square, or octagonal serving as police-stations, prisons, or lookouts, by bath or circus, in the shipyards and wharves of the Golden Horn, were swarms of people. The Greeks in their robes of wool or silk were almost lost in the crowd of barbarians or semi-barbarians, their national dress relieved sometimes by some tawdrier trinket of Byzantine craft: Bulgars with their close-cropped hair and copper belts; Russians 'tall as palm-trees'; turbaned Persians; Nubian negroes; Hungarians; Khazars; Jewish mer-

Plan of Constantinople drawn by Giovanni Vavassore about 1520.

chants from Palestine; Franks and Italians; pilgrims from the whole Christian world. Here in a public square a monk would be held in argument by a motley group of citizens (had not Gregory of Nyssa some centuries earlier already remarked on the speculative genius of the Constantinopolitan: *The city is full of mechanics and slaves who are all of them profound theologians, and they preach in the shops and the streets. If you want a man to change a piece of money for you he informs you of in what the Son differs from the Father; if you ask the price of a loaf you are told by way of reply that the Son is inferior to the Father; and if you inquire whether the bath is ready, the answer is that the Son was begotten out of nothing.*) Further on, Arabian acrobats dance on a rope, Indians parade an elephant. A court dignitary, in costume of brocaded silk, passes on horseback, a long cortège behind him. A procession files past. Nuns veiled in white, enveloped in black shawls, bearing an icon of the Panaghia in their midst, precede a group of priests, censers in hand, robed in their brocaded dalmatics, in stoles red or green and sewn with a golden cross. Students from the Imperial University turned over books in the book-vendors' stalls set up in front of the Basilica, seat of the law-courts. A carriage drawn by four white horses, their harness encrusted with gold and silver, and

13

bearing some great nobleman or favoured courtier, passes a lumbering Scythian coach, its passengers clothed in skins. Nor did this movement cease with sunset, for the main areas of the city had been lit since the fourth century, and in such a place as the Palace of Lamps, a great vaulted bazaar, a forest of lights burnt on late into the night. Here the city's richest merchants displayed their wares: brocades with figures raised in relief, cups of onyx, glass-ware set with enamel, perfumes of India and Arabia, ornamental vases whose paintings illustrated the main Christian legends, silver reliquaries studded with *cabochon* jewels, illuminated manuscripts: all those items, religious and profane, which, spread by Italian and Jewish merchants through the castles and cloisters of France and England, the burgs of the Rhine, the palaces of Italy, rejoiced the heart of prelate, chatelaine, and cavalier alike.

But everywhere within this intense and continuous movement were pools of quiet, centres of withdrawal within the city's maelstrom, enclosed spaces free from prying eye and extraneous distraction, given over to the practice of prayer and contemplation. In an age in which, as it has been said, the degradation of the inner life is amply demonstrated by the fact that the only place secure from intrusion in our modern urban agglomerations is the lavatory, it is difficult to imagine the impact which the presence in its midst of monastery and convent must have had on the medieval city. And at Constantinople the number of such organized shelters from worldly importunity was legion. Here in cloister and walled garden the liberating round of the monastic discipline continued day and night at the very heart of the city, perpetual reminder of the superb vanity of the spectacle which ran its mundane course outside their gates. Yet it is precisely when it is challenged in this way, at its very heart, that this spectacle, this collective expression of the human ego, achieves, as at Constantinople, the quality of a moving pageant or of a dance renewed continually on the brink of its own denial. Where this ever-present repudiation of its most cherished claims, this sense of the perpetual judgement of all its ephemeral preoccupations, is banished from the city, as it is banished from the modern city, then the spectacle of the city's life itself sinks to the ultimate drabness of an army camp whose pleasure- or profit-bound conscripts gyrate in the vortex of their own soul-destroying fatuity. The least that can be said in this connexion is that it is not architects, engineers, or plumbers that can make a city human, and that they labour in vain who build it where the spirit, invoked in prayer, is not a vital concern of the citizens. Where Constantinople, and indeed the whole Byzantine world, is concerned, one has to remember that all the complexity and variety of its manifold forms flowered against and from this invisible background of ceaseless prayer.

Not that this complexity and variety in Constantinople itself was in any case merely haphazard, merely the result of a fratricidal struggle of private enterprise in which each pursues his own gain at the expense of his neighbour. On the contrary, behind it lay a strict discipline of economic and civic control. Here all was regulated, all determined according to an established pattern. *Having created all things and made order and harmony reign in the world*, ran the Emperor's preface to the manual of the city's internal organization, 'The Book of the Prefect', *God engraved the Law with his own finger on the Tables, and set it forth for all to see so that it might prevent by a happy discipline the members of the human family from hurling themselves one upon the other and the stronger from crushing the weaker. He desired that all should be weighed among them with a just balance. It is for this reason that it has appeared good to our Serenity also to formulate the dispositions which result from the law, so that the human race is governed as is fitting and so that one person does not oppress another.*[5] It was in this spirit that the whole of the city's economic life was organized on the basis of strictly controlled guilds or corporations, one for each trade and all under the constant and meticulous supervision of the State. Of this organization the chief official was the Prefect, or Eparch, of the city: it was to him that the corporations and their members and all their affairs were subordinate. Their recruitment, the election of their senior officers, their mutual relationships, and their whole existence depended on him; it was he who represented them *vis-à-vis* the government and, in most cases,

Ear-pendant of the sixth or seventh century from Constantinople.

Table of Eusebian Canons from a Byzantine gospel-book of the beginning of the eleventh century. Bibliothèque Nationale, Paris.

vis-à-vis the foreign population of the city; and it was he who judged and punished infringements of their intricate regulations. Superior to him was of course the Emperor who nominated him, invested him with the insignia of his office, and could at any moment relieve him of his duties. But as long as he held office he was the virtual master of the city, the executor of its laws, its chief of police, regulator of its commercial and human traffic.

Though subject to the formal approval of the Prefect, admission to the corporations was on a hereditary basis, or could, in certain circumstances, be conferred by marriage: 'If someone takes a wife from the class of shell-fishers', runs the imperial code, 'let him know that he will himself be attached to the same class.' Once admitted, each member had to pursue his own speciality: the goldsmith could concern himself only with gold, candle-makers with candles, soap-makers with soap, the makers of scent were restricted to trade in spices: pepper from the Indies, spikenard from Laodicea, cinnamon from Asia and Ceylon, aloes from China, Java, and Sumatra, musk from Tibet, incense, myrrh, and balsam from Arabia, 'sweet-smelling beet', *lazonray* (purgative or seasoning), and ambergris from the East. There were no intermediaries: each member was in direct contact with his clientèle and offered his products direct to consumers. He assumed all charges and carried all risks, though prices were fixed by tariff, weights and measures were controlled, profits were limited. He was the proprietor of the articles he fabricated, and to him belonged the tools, raw materials, and the capital for exploitation which he needed. On the other hand, he could only exercise his trade in a particular quarter of the town, though 'grocers may have a shop anywhere'; he had to fulfil certain public functions, police and other; and his workshop, his stall, his books were at any moment liable to the most rigorous examination.

Independent of this guild-organization designed to meet the needs of the populace was the State itself, which, to meet its own vast needs, had its own enterprises. It monopolized the purchase of silk and reserved the best qualities for its own manufacture. It undertook most public works—the building of palaces, fortifications, aqueducts, roads. It reserved certain dyes for imperial use: 'Dyers', ran the ordinance, 'are forbidden to make up the purple of the so-called prohibited grades, that is to say in the series of great mantles, including those of self colour or those where the purple alternates with dark green or yellow in half-tint'. It acted as a giant and privileged entrepreneur: to furnish the court the corporations were compelled to provide their services and to work without contract, with buying conditions and prices fixed by high court functionaries. Above all, it owned and controlled the mints, those mints from which issued that symbol of the unalterable integrity of the imperial power, the unalloyed gold bezant of full weight. It was this gold coinage that, in a discordant and unstable world, stood as the Empire's gage of universal trust and security. The story is told of the Byzantine merchant Zopatros, who, trading in the East, demonstrated the superiority of his Emperor over the Persian autocrat by showing to the king of Ceylon the unmatched splendour of the bezant; and when the Venerable Bede wishes to praise a British princess he does so by calling her as pure as one of these untarnished coins. To this golden magnet were drawn the *lazzaroni* of Europe and Asia alike, seeking commercial favours from the imperial government; and under its spell Jews and Moslems, Russians and Italians, Syrians from Babylon and Palestine, Persians and Egyptians, Patzinaks (Pechenegs) and Bulgars, Lombards and Spaniards, Georgians, Armenians, and Turks crowded the narrow alleys and broad thoroughfares of the capital, giving the city a cosmopolitanism that embraced distinctions of race and religion (had not the Moslems, for instance, an official mosque, where, to the horror of the Crusaders, their resident and visiting faithful could worship freely?), and bringing to it a wealth which, according to a western witness, Robert de Clari,[6] the forty richest cities of the world could not exceed. *Vous pouvez savoir qu'ils regardèrent beaucoup Constantinople ceux qui jamais ne l'avaient vue*, wrote Villehardouin; *car ils ne pouvaient penser qu'il pût être en tout le monde une si riche ville, quand ils virent ces hauts murs et ces riches tours dont elle était close tout entour à la ronde, et ces riches palais et ces hautes églises dont il y avait tant que nul ne le pût croire s'il ne l'eût vu de ses yeux....*[7]

*

Constantius II as Consul, distributing largesse. From the Calendar of A.D. 354.

Outwardly, the press and turbulence of the rich life of the Byzantine capital revolved round the three great structures or groups of buildings that shared the central tableland and the southern and eastern slopes of the final hill of the promontory on which the city stood: the Hippodrome, the Sacred Imperial Palace, and the great Church of St. Sophia. Lying between them, on the crest of the hill, was the main public square, the Augustaeum, an open rectangular court paved with slabs of dark-coloured marble and surrounded by an interior arcade or peristyle. Its outer wall was pierced by a number of gateways, the two most important being the one leading into St. Sophia to the north and the corresponding one to the south leading out into the Mesê and hence into the Palace. It was in this great square that the Emperor, after he had passed through this latter gate on his way to St. Sophia for his coronation, used to be raised aloft on a shield by his nobles and acclaimed by the populace. It was in this square also that, on a rectangular stepped base of stone, whose successive courses could be used for seats, stood the huge bronze equestrian statue of Justinian, monument to the Emperor's pride. Made of large blocks of stone in circular courses, cut so as to form angles on their inner faces and fitted together by the skill of the masons, the entire column was sheathed in bronze, the latter banded at various intervals by a wreath motif in relief. *And this bronze*, says Procopius, *is in tone softer than pure gold, and its value little less than that of an equal weight in silver.* And Procopius continues: *And at the top of the column stands a huge bronze horse which*

17

*faces the East and is a noble sight. He looks as if he is advancing, pressing forward magnificently, his left forefoot
in the air as though about to be placed on the ground in front, the right on the stone where he stands, based for the
next step; while he holds the hind legs together, ready for wherever they must next be moved. On this horse is a
huge statue of the Emperor, dressed like Achilles—at least, the costume he has on is known by this name. He
wears boots but no greaves, and his breastplate is in the heroic style; while the helmet covering his head seems to
move up and down (with the horse's movement), and it gleams dazzlingly. Using poetic language, one might
say that here is the star of Autumn. He looks towards the rising sun, riding, it seems to me, toward the Persians.
In his left hand he carries a globe, the sculptor signifying by this that all earth and sea are subject to him, though
he has neither sword nor spear nor other weapon, except that on the globe stands the cross through which alone he
has achieved his kingdom and his mastery in war.* [8]

It was to the south of the Augustaeum that lay that great mirror of Constantinopolitan popular life,
the Hippodrome. First built by the Emperor Septimius Severus in the third century, and in its completed
form said to be capable of seating some 60,000 spectators, its arched walls, of marble filled with brick,
rose some forty feet from the ground to support a colonnade of gigantic marble pillars from whose bases
tier upon tier of white marble seats sloped down to the arena. The semi-circular curve at the south-
western end, also tiered with seats, over-reached the flat tableland of the hill and was strutted up on
massive vaults. Down the centre of the arena ran the *spina*, or backbone, a barrier on which had been
placed some of the major works of ancient art of which Constantinople had become the repository, two
of the chief being, first, a great Egyptian monolithic obelisk of porphyry eighty-four feet high, which
still stands on its sculptured base showing the Emperor presiding at the games; and, second, the bronze
column already mentioned, the heads of whose three snakes spouting from their long intertwined necks
had once borne the gold tripod dedicated to Apollo after the Greek victory at Plataea. At the blunt north-
eastern end of the arena rose the imperial tribune, the *kathisma*, inaccessible from the Hippodrome but
linked directly with the Palace, and the boxes of the high dignitaries with, beneath them, stables and
vestibules for horse and chariot. It was from here that the Emperor and members of his court (though
not the Empress, for she had her seat in the women's gallery of one of the palatine churches bordering
the Hippodrome, from which she could watch unseen by the crowds)—it was from here that the Emperor
and high dignitaries could look down on the seething, often turbulent mass of spectators, whether
gathered for the celebration of chariot races and public games, the execution of a criminal, or the return
of a triumphant general from the battle-front.

It was of course for chariot races that the Hippodrome was primarily intended, and it was these that
remained for the citizens of Constantinople the main focus of their popular concern and passion. Indeed,
their whole organization and conduct involved what were the most important citizen bodies of the
capital, the factions. These had originally been four in number—the Greens, Blues, Reds, and Whites—
though gradually for all effective purposes the Greens (*prasins*) absorbed the Reds, and the Blues
(*venets*) absorbed the Whites. It was said that Romulus had first given the factions their colours, though
historically their appearance coincides with that of the absolutism of the Roman Emperor, after the
Republic: Caligula, for instance, was an ardent supporter of the Greens, as was Nero; Vitellius supported
the Blues. Established in Constantinople on the same lines as those of Rome, the factions became so
powerful that the government found it necessary to organize them in a quasi-political fashion. Named
the *demes* (from *dêmos*, the people), they took on the form of a club run something on the lines of local
militia. Each faction had its leader, the demarch, who was responsible to the administration, and beneath
him was a whole hierarchy of dignitaries, employees, treasurers, notaries, archivists, heralds, poets,
musicians, organists of the choir, painters and sculptors, charioteers and circus-performers for
the intervals between races, officials for keeping order in the Hippodrome, stable-hands, and others.

CONSTANTINOPLE

Scutari

porta aurea

S. Sophia

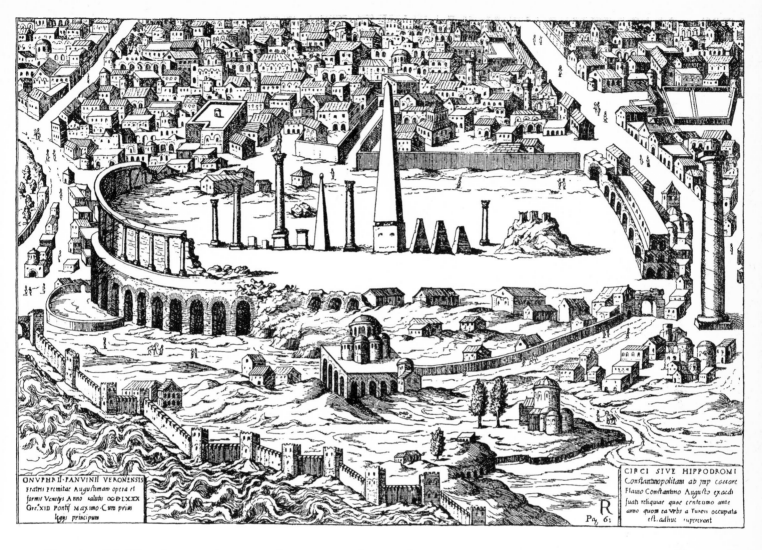

The ruins of the Hippodrome, as they appeared in A.D. 1450, after Onophrius Panvinius of Verona.

Illustration opposite: Relief from the pedestal of the Obelisk in the Hippodrome, showing the Emperor watching the games in the Hippodrome from his box. He holds in his hand the wreath destined for the victor; dignitaries and body-guards surround him; below him is the crowd of spectators, and, in front of the arena, musicians and dancing-girls. End of the fourth century: Istanbul.

Below: Enlargement of part of a miniature representing a chariot-race. From an illustrated Iliad of the fifth or sixth century, probably produced at Constantinople and now in the Ambrosian Library at Milan.

Moreover, the activities of the factions were by no means restricted to chariot-racing. Along with this quasi-political organization they also assumed a quasi-political role. They were armed and could be called on to defend the walls of the city. They escorted the Emperor in his cavalcades through the city or on pilgrimages to the various churches. They lined the streets during processions or festivals and proclaimed the official acclamations or pieces of verse prepared for the occasion. They composed and recited the epithalamiums at the Emperor's marriage and they accompanied the Empress on her way to the bath she had by tradition to take three days after her marriage. On days prescribed by the ceremonial for entertainment, delegates of the factions would be invited to the Palace, to take part in the festivities, to accompany the gothic dances with songs and tambourines. They sported outlandish clothes: cloaks and shoes of the barbarian Huns, tunics with wide billowing sleeves fastened at the wrist by a ribbon; and they wore moustaches and beards and a bizarre hair-style, close-cropping the hair on the fore-part of the head and letting it grow long and hang down, Persian fashion, at the back.

But it was in the Hippodrome itself that the political role of the factions was most explicit. For the Hippodrome was not only a race-course; it was also the setting for the expression of popular feeling and liberties; for executions and brandings; for the gouging out of eyes and the slitting of noses. It was here that the Emperor Maurice (582–602) felt the support of the crowd withdrawn from him at the approach of the centurion Phocas, his future assassin and successor; it was here that the tyrant Justinian II (685–695 and 705–711), prisoner of rebels, had his nose and ears cut off; and it was here too that later, when he returned from exile, he trod with his scarlet buskins on the heads of his defeated enemies before sending them to their death, while the crowd, fickle as it was savage, angry as it could be gay, cried out: 'You tread on the asp and the basilisk.' It was here that the Emperor Michael Calaphates (1041–1042), having exiled his adoptive mother and protectress, was attacked with arrows and stones in his royal box; and here the tyrant Andronicus Comnenus (1183–1185) received his terrible punishment. But perhaps the most ferocious demonstration of popular passion or imperial vengeance was that which took place in the reign of Justinian, when discontent against a corrupt and exacting officialdom came to a head in a riot organized by the factions—the famous Nika Rebellion, so-called after the people's battle-cry of 'nika, nika!', 'conquer, conquer!' The purpose of the revolt was to depose Justinian and to overthrow his unpopular finance minister, John the Cappadocian. Learning of this, Justinian, carrying a copy of the Gospels in his hands, appeared in the Hippodrome and swore he would grant an amnesty and satisfy the people's demands. But the crowd remained hostile and unappeased. After burning half the original city of Constantine to the ground, they crowned a pretender as Emperor in the Forum of Constantine, took him to the Hippodrome, and seated him as Emperor in the imperial box. Justinian prepared to flee; and the situation was only saved by the courage of the Empress Theodora and the efficiency of the imperial guards, detachments of which, penetrating into the Hippodrome, left what contemporary accounts estimate as 30,0000 of the rioters lying dead among the marble seats. Their mass grave was near one of the gates hereafter known as the Nekra gate, the gate of Death.

The Nika Rebellion was of course an exception, and other occasions on which the political passions of the Hippodrome crowd developed under the leadership of the factions to the point of uncontrollable violence were relatively few. But the threat was always there, and unwise was the Emperor who refused to listen to the people's voice as it was given expression by one or other of the Hippodrome factions, whether its concern was for cheaper oil, fewer taxes, or the life of a cruel and unjust minister. Normally the petition or grievance could be conveyed through a spokesman of the faction maintaining it, who, standing in front of the imperial box, was allowed to hold a dialogue with an imperial herald who spoke for the Emperor. Sometimes, though, a more ingenious method would be found. Once, in the reign of the Emperor Theophilus (829–842), the prefect of the Palace stole a galley and all its cargo from a widow. The widow sought redress from the legal authorities, but without success. Finally she turned to one of the pantomimes that entertained the Hippodrome audiences between the races. The players built a miniature boat, and, placing themselves beneath the imperial box, conducted the following dialogue: 'Come, swallow this little ship for me!'—'Impossible!'—'Impossible? Why? The palace prefect can devour a whole galley with its cargo and you can't swallow this black shell?' The Emperor, intrigued, sent for further information, learnt of what had happened, and, while the Hippodrome was still in session, placed the guilty functionary, clothed in his official court regalia and costume, on a pyre and burnt him alive before the terror-struck populace.

Yet although chariot-racing was not the only, it was the main function of the Hippodrome. The passion of the Byzantines for this sport had all the uncouth frenzy that in the modern age is reserved for football matches. There was indeed a veritable cult both of horses and of charioteers which infected Emperor and populace alike. Though no single Byzantine horse has achieved the notoriety of Caligula's Incitatus, appointed consul by his imperial owner, yet Constantinople may claim that she produced, in the person of the Patriarch Theophylact, what is perhaps the supreme example of hippic lunacy of all time. A rival in the arts of debauchery of his exalted and contemporary compeers, the Popes John XI and John XII, this venerable ecclesiastic, son of an Emperor and raised to the oecumenical throne at the extraordinary age of sixteen, possessed a stable, palatial in its white marble, of some thousand horses, which he fed on corn, pistachio nuts, dates, and raisins, washed in the finest wines, and perfumed with saffron and cinnamon. The story is told of how this Patriarch, informed while officiating at the altar of St. Sophia before Emperor and court, prelates and people, of the accouchement of a favourite mare, left all and hurried to her side, to return to the church after a successful delivery in time to take part in the final procession of the liturgy. After twenty-three years on the patriarchal throne, Theophylact ended his life at the foot of the wall against which he had been thrown from the back of one of his unmanageable steeds. A similar addiction possessed the Emperor Michael III (842–867); wearing the ensign of the Blues, he took the reins of his own chariot in his private Hippodrome. When on one occasion the attention of the crowd was withdrawn from the racing by the sight of a beacon, last of a line that stretched from the

Chariot-race with quadrigas. Section of a Roman mosaic on the Via Imperiale.

depths of Asia Minor, burning on a hill above the Bosphorus and signifying the defeat of the imperial armies on the banks of the Euphrates, Michael in his anger ordered the extinction of the beacon and the continuation of the race. After his assassination by Basil I the Macedonian, who hailed from his own stables, his mutilated body was found wrapped in a horse-cloth.

The real heroes of the Hippodrome were, however, the charioteers. Possessing their own grades and insignia—a certificate signed with red imperial ink, a belt round the loins, a silver-embroidered cap— and by virtue of their profession entitled to certain privileges and exceptions, they were the adored idols of the team-torn, screaming Byzantine crowd as it rocked in its seats to the thundering hooves. Statues in their honour were set up in the Hippodrome and other public places. On the pedestals of some of these there were verse inscriptions:

Constantinus deserved a golden gift for his merit, since his art has produced none like him. While a youth he overcame the celebrated drivers, and in his old age showed that the young were his inferiors.

Or again, on one of the most famous of all the charioteers:

Porphyrius, wonder of the Blues, having defeated every charioteer on earth, does well to rise and race towards heaven. For he, victorious over every driver here below, mounts to join the sun on its course.

Or, poignant in its brevity:

Since Constantinus has entered Hades' hall all the glory of charioteering has gone with him.

In such a way did the Byzantines express their worship of their beloved heroes of the Hippodrome.

Flanking the Hippodrome to the east and also fronting on the Augustaeum was the Sacred Palace, residence of the Emperor. This vast and rambling cluster of buildings with gardens, terraces, isolated summer pavilions, churches, reception halls, private stadium, indoor riding school, polo-ground, swimming-baths, fountains, with their accompanying complex of storerooms, kitchens, stables, servants' quarters, guard-rooms, and dungeons, covered the woody slopes of the eastern and south-eastern end of the city's promontory down to the Sea of Marmara and the Bosphorus. It was entered through a monumental vestibule off the south-east corner of the Augustaeum, at the terminus of the Mesê, the main thoroughfare of the city. This building, the Chalkê—Brazen, for its roof and doors were of gilded bronze—was rebuilt after the Nika Rebellion by Justinian and further restored in the ninth century by the Emperor Basil the Macedonian (867–886). Procopius gives a description of it as it was after it had been rebuilt by Justinian: *The entrance, called the Chalkê, is as follows. Four tall upright walls form a quadrangle, each similar to the other except that those to the south and north are slightly shorter. At each corner there is a kind of projection of finely worked stones which goes from the ground to the top of the wall; it is four-sided (one side being joined to the wall) and not only doesn't spoil the beauty of the room but adds to it through the harmony of its similar proportions. Eight arches rise over them, four supporting the roof which curves dome-like over the centre, while the others, two to the south and two to the north, are joined to the adjacent walls, and lift up the vaulted roof between them. The whole roof is covered with pictures, not congealed from wax which has been melted and poured over it, but set in tiny stones of many beautiful colours, representing human beings and other things as I shall now describe. On either side is war and battle, and many cities being taken, some in Italy, some in Libya: the Emperor Justinian conquering through his general, Belisarius, who is coming back to the Emperor with his whole army intact and presenting him a booty of kings and kingdoms and all things esteemed by men. The Emperor and the Empress Theodora stand in the centre, both seeming to rejoice and to be celebrating the triumph over the kings of the Vandals and the Goths who draw near as prisoners of war being led into captivity. Round them stands the Roman senate, also in festive mood, the mosaics showing the joy shining in their faces. They exult and smile, according the Emperor god-like honour for the great things he has done. The whole of the inside, up to the mosaics—not merely the upright surfaces but the floor as well—, is dressed with fine marbles, some of the Spartan stone, challenging the emerald, some simulating the fire's flame, though most are white, not plain white, but white mixed with wavy lines of blue. So much, then, for this.*[9]

In the Chalkê also stood a whole host of statues: of the Empress Pulcheria; of Zeus and Ariadne; and of many others. In the vault opposite the bronze door were the four Gorgons' heads from the temple of Diana at Ephesus, and above them, also brought from Ephesus by Justinian, two bronze horses.

Behind the Chalkê was the Tribunal of the Nineteen Couches (*accubita*), the large reception hall in which official banquets were held. Beyond this again were other palaces and halls: the Hall of Pearl, with its eight columns of Rhodian marble and its walls covered with paintings of animals; the Camilas, its roof supported on six columns of green Thessalian marble and the upper part of its walls decorated with gold-ground mosaics of men and women plucking fruit; the Mousikos, with its seven columns of Carian marble and its walls a harmony of multi-coloured marble slabs. One of the most dazzling of all the buildings was the Chrysotriclinos, the hall of gold, an octagonal structure whose dome, pierced by sixteen windows, was supported on eight columns and as many arches. The eastern arch opened on to an apse where, beneath the image of the enthroned Christ, stood the imperial throne, visible representation of the royal power imaged above. When the Emperor took his seat on the throne his retinue formed in a semi-circle behind him. Before the throne was a great curtain of silk woven with gold and ornamented with precious stones. The other furnishings of the hall were equally lavish: further imperial thrones, couches, a great gold banqueting table, engraved plates, crowns, objects in enamel, chandeliers, crosses, imperial vestments, many of these contained in the huge cupboard, the Pentapyrgion, built in five tiers, two golden and bejewelled organs, silver doors. Another equally sumptuous palace was the Magnaura, with the famous reception hall containing the 'throne of Solomon', so-called because of its alleged likeness to this latter. The throne was reached by six steps; on each side of it stood golden lions, and above it rose trees of gilded bronze in whose branches glittered jewelled and enamelled birds. When at a reception the Emperor ascended his throne, then 'the instruments sounded and, as the chamberlain put to him the usual inquiries, the lions began to roar and the birds on the throne to sing in harmony, as did also those in the trees; and the animals worked upon the throne rose up, each in its own place'.[10]

Two of the most splendid buildings of the whole group were added in the latter part of the ninth century by the Emperor Basil I the Macedonian. The first was the New Palace, a basilica-like building supported on a magnificent colonnade in which eight columns of verd-antique alternated with eight of red onyx decorated with reliefs of vines and animals. On the walls and ceiling were huge compositions in mosaic showing Basil I receiving from his generals the gifts of captured cities and recounting the Herculean exploits of the Emperor. On the floor of the imperial bedchamber nearby, strips of Carian marble radiated outward from the mosaic peacock framed in a central medallion of the same marble until they met the circumference of a larger circle. From this in turn ran to the four corners of the room four streams of green marble, enclosing in the spaces between them four eagles, their mosaic plumage stretched ready for flight. Beneath the wainscotting of gold reliefs the walls with their plaques of multi-coloured glass shimmered like a field of flowers. Above the wainscotting, the imperial family—the Emperor with his wife and children, ceremonially apparelled—were ranged on a background of gold, their hands raised towards the brilliant green cross in the centre of the ceiling. The inscription bore the words of the parents: 'We thank you, most good God, King of kings, that you have surrounded us with children who give thanks to you for your bounty. Keep them according to your will. May none of them transgress your commandments, so that for this too we may give thanks for your goodness'; and of the children: 'We thank you, Word of God, that you have raised our father from the poverty of David and have anointed him with your Spirit. Guard him and our mother with your hand, that they with us may be judged worthy of the heavenly kingdom.'[11]

So, like the Emperor and his lady themselves, one could wander for ever between the walls of marble and gold, crushing the scent of flowers and herbs, opening the doors of silver and ivory, brushing the scarlet curtains woven with animals, dazzled by the long vistas of carpets and chandeliers; through the palatine churches, the small chapel of the Saviour by the Chalkê, the church of Our Lady of the Pharos, the *capella palatina* above all others, its capitals and cornices adorned with gold, the New Church of Basil I with its five domes glowing in the sun and the water from the two fountains outside its western façade spouting through the mouths of bronze cocks, goats, and rams; past the many other fountains, the 'Mystic Phiale' of the Sigma expelling its wine through a golden pineapple into a silver-bound basin full of almonds and pistachios; past the porphyry chamber reserved for the accouchement of the Empresses, the polo-ground where young gallants managed their restive mounts, pools whose broad-leaved nenuphars shaded coloured fish; along walks baked by the hot summer sun; down the monumental stairways to where, in the artificial harbour of the Boucoleon, the royal yachts and barges lay at anchor. Here was a promenade, there a bridge over a running stream, here a pavilion, rendezvous on the long summer evenings of the many sweet colours and sounds that graced this haven over the still waters of the Bosphorus.

*

The third main building sharing with the Hippodrome and the Sacred Palace the narrow tableland athwart the first hill of the city's promontory was the great church of St. Sophia, once the very heart of the whole Byzantine world, and still, though degraded to the status of a museum, a supreme artistic expression of the Christian consciousness. Standing to the north-east of the Augustaeum, the original church was built, on foundations laid by Constantine the Great, by the latter's son, Constantius, and on 15 February 360 was dedicated to the Immortal Wisdom of Christ—Ἀθανατῷ Σοφίᾳ τοῦ Χριστοῦ. 'For the opening ceremony', adds the chronicle, 'Constantius brought many offerings of gold and great treasure of silver; many fabrics adorned with gold thread and stones for the sanctuary; for the doors of the church various hangings of gold; and for the outer gates many others with gold threads.'[12] In 404, however, partisans of St. John Chrysostom, banished from the city because of the enmity of the Empress Eudoxia, set fire to this original church and largely destroyed it. It was rebuilt, but was again burnt on the first day of the Nika Rebellion in January 532. In the following month Justinian began the work of reconstruction. Procopius has left a brief account of the undertaking: *Men of the common herd, mere refuse, rising against the Emperor Justinian in Byzantium, brought about the revolt called the Nika Rebellion.... And as though showing they'd taken up arms not simply against the Emperor, but against God as well, unspeakable people, they set fire to the church of the Christians which the Byzantines call 'Sophia', an epithet they apply most fittingly to God. God allowed them to carry out this infamy, foreseeing by what beauty his temple was to be transformed. The church then was a heap of ashes. But not long afterwards the Emperor Justinian so magnificently wrought it, that if one had asked the Christians earlier whether they'd have liked the church to be destroyed and this one put in its place (showing them a model of the present building), I'm sure they'd have prayed to have their church destroyed at once, so that it might be changed to its present form. The Emperor then, regardless of expense, pressed on with the building, gathering artisans from everywhere. And Anthemius of Tralles, most skilled in the builder's art not only among the living, but also of those who had been before him, served the Emperor's eagerness, ordering the artisans' tasks and preparing models of the future building. With him was another master-builder, Isodorus, a Milesian, also intelligent and fit to serve the Emperor Justinian. This too was part of the honour God showed the Emperor, providing him with those most suitable for carrying out the tasks to be done. And one might also admire the Emperor's good sense in this, that for his major undertakings he was able to select out of all the men available those best equipped for the work in hand.* [13]

Within six years the building was dedicated. At last the holy morn had come, wrote Paul the Silentiary, contemporary poet, of this second dedication, *and the great door of the new-built temple groaned on its opening hinges, inviting Emperor and people to enter; and when the inner part was seen sorrow fled from the hearts of all, as the sun lit the glories of the temple. It was for the Emperor to lead the way for his people, and on the morrow to celebrate the birth of Christ. And when the first gleam of light rosy-armed driving away the dark shadows leapt from arch to arch, then all the princes and people with one voice hymned their songs of prayer and praise; and as they came to the sacred courts, it seemed to them as if the mighty arches were set in heaven.* [14] Entering the church at this dedication, Justinian walked alone down its length till he came to the pulpit. There he raised his hands to heaven and cried: 'Glory be to God, who has thought me worthy to finish this work. Solomon, I have outdone thee!'

Except for the dome, rebuilt after an earthquake in 558, the essential structure of the church as it stood at the time of dedication in 537 still stands today. As Procopius rightly says, no expense was spared to make this building the consummate performance of stone and light and space which it is. Entering through one of the three doors (commemorative of the Trinity) that lead from the narthex, the main body of the church 'lies open forming an immense space, having a hollowness so spacious that it might be pregnant with many thousands of bodies and a height so great as to turn the head, and make the eyes stop still as it were at the zenith'. [15] Paving this space and panelling its walls were sheet upon sheet of marble, cut and cut again so that the veining of each piece should merge with that of its neighbour, alternating with bands of other marbles set in delicately notched bevelling. *Yet who*, sang the Silentiary, *who even in the measures of Homer shall sing the marble pastures gathered on the lofty walls and spreading pavement of the mighty church? Those the iron with its metal tooth has gnawed—the fresh green from Carystus, polychrome marble from the Phrygian range, in which a rosy blush mingles with white, or it shines bright with flowers of deep red and silver. There is a wealth of porphyry too, powdered with bright stars, that has once laden the river boat on the broad Nile. You would see an emerald green from Sparta, and the glittering marble with wavy veins which the tool has worked in the deep breast of the Iassian hills, showing slanting streaks blood-red and livid white. From the Lydian creek came the bright stone mingled with streaks of red. Stone too there is that the Libyan sun, warming with his golden light, has nourished in the deep clefts of the hills of the Moors, of crocus colour glittering like gold; and the product of the Celtic crags, a wealth of crystals, like milk poured here and there on a flesh of glittering black. There is the precious onyx, as if gold were shining through it; and the marble that the land of Atrax yields, not from some upland glen, but from the level plains; in parts fresh green as the sea or emerald stone, or again like blue cornflowers in grass, with here and there a drift of fallen snow—a sweet mingled contrast on the dark shining surface.*

A curving row of pillars, porphyry, verd-antique, of every kind of marble, rise from the pavement up to the gilded capitals, whence spring arches that carry the galleries. Here another curving row of pillars, similarly sprung with arches, support the upper walls, wrought in a texture of punctured elaboration, inset with plaques of porphyry. Then, as the eye is carried forward (we speak now of the church of imperial times), gradually it reaches where the four triangular pendentives, each with its mosaic of flame-like six-winged cherubim, curve gently outwards to support the cornice of the dome which 'seems not to rest upon solid masonry but to cover the space beneath as though suspended from heaven'. [16]

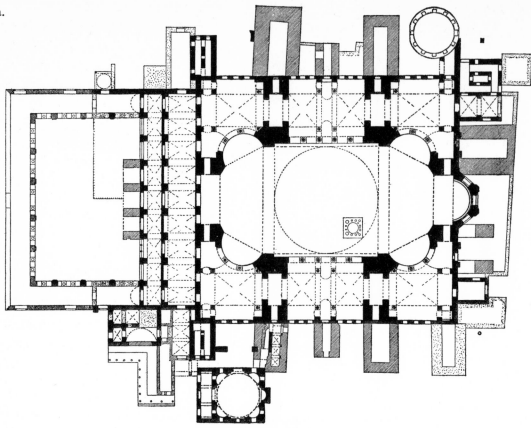

Hence, from a ground of gold, originally a cross, later the image of the Christ Pantocrator himself looks down in majesty. On the pavement beneath him stands the ambo, a huge jasper pulpit borne on eight pillars and inlaid with ivory and silver. Two stairways descend from this to a passage, banistered in verd-antique, which leads to the iconostasis, the great screen closing off the sanctuary of the eastern apse. *For as much of the great church by the eastern arch was set apart for the bloodless sacrifice—it is again Paul the Silentiary who speaks—no ivory, no stone, nor bronze distinguishes, but it is all fenced with the silver metal. Not only upon the walls, which separate the holy priests from the crowd of singers, has he placed mere plates of silver, but he has covered all the columns themselves with the silver metal, even six sets of twain; and the rays of light glitter far and wide. Upon them the tool has formed dazzling circles, beautifully wrought in skilled symmetry by the craftsman's hand, in the centre of which is carved the symbol of the Immaculate God, who took upon Himself the form of man. In parts stands up an army of winged angels in pairs, with bent necks and downcast mien (for they could not gaze upon the glory of the Godhead, though hidden in the form of man to clean man's flesh from sin). And elsewhere the tool has fashioned the heralds of the way of God, even those by whose words were spread abroad, before He took flesh upon Him, the divine tidings of the Anointed One. Nor had the craftsman forgotten the forms of those others, whose childhood was with the fishing-basket and the net, but who left the mean labours of life and unholy cares to bear witness at the bidding of a heavenly king, fishing even for men, and forsaking the skill of casting nets to weave the beauteous seine of eternal life. In other parts art has represented the Mother of Christ, the vessel of eternal Light, whose womb brought Him forth in holy travail. But on the middle panels of the sacred screen, which forms the barrier for the priests, the carver's art has cut one letter that means many words, for it*

Illustration opposite: View of the nave of St. Sophia from a gallery. The painting of the vaults is of Turkish origin, as are the four great roundels with names in the choir, the prayer-niche, the railings, and the lights.

28

combines the name of our king and queen. And he has also wrought a form like a shield with a boss, showing the cross in the middle parts. And through the triple doors the screen opens to the priests. For on each side the skilful hand of the workman has made small doors.

Within these doors, in the holy of holies, stands the 'wonder of all nations', the holy table, a slab of gold inlaid with precious stones and supported by four golden columns. Above it *rises in the air a tower indescribable, supported on fourfold arches of silver. And it is borne aloft on silver columns, on whose tops every arch rests its silver feet. And above the arches rises a figure like a cone, yet it is not complete. For at the bottom its edge does not turn round in the circular form, but has an eight-sided base, and from a broad plan it gradually diminishes to a sharp point, having eight sides of silver. And where one side meets another there is as it were a long backbone which seems to join with the triangular faces of the eight-sided form, and rises to a single crest, where the form of a cup is artfully fashioned. And the edges of the cup bend over and take the form of leaves, and in the midst of it has been placed a shining silver globe, and the cross surmounts it all. May it be an omen of peace!* [17]

Figure of Christ from a Byzantine enamel of the twelfth century in the Biblioteca Marciana, Venice.

Red curtains bearing the woven figures of Christ flanked by St. Peter and St. Paul hung round the altar and its overshadowing ciborium. The central figure of Christ wore *a garment shimmering with gold, like the rays of the rosy-fingered dawn, which flashes down to the divine knees, and a chiton, deep red from the Tyrian shell dye, covers the right shoulder.... The upper robe has slipped away and pulled up across the side it only covers the left shoulder while the forearm and the hand are bare. He seems to point the fingers of the right hand, as if preaching the Words of Life, and in the left hand He holds the Book of the Divine Message—the Book that tells what the Messiah accomplished when his foot was on the earth. And the whole robe shines with gold; for on it a thin gold thread is led through the web.... And on either side stand the two messengers of God—Paul, full of divine wisdom, and also the mighty doorkeeper of the Gates of Heaven, binding with both heavenly and earthly chains. One holds the Book pregnant with sacred words, and the other the form of a cross on a staff of gold. The cunning web has clothed both in robes of silver white.... On the borders of the curtain, indescribable art has figured the works of mercy of our City's rulers; here one sees hospitals for the sick, there sacred churches, while on either side are displayed the miracles of Christ.... But on the other curtains you see the kings of the earth, on one side with their hands joined to those of Our Lady, on the other side joined to those of Christ, and all is cunningly wrought by the threads of the woof with the sheen of a golden warp....* [18]

It was round the curtained altar that the Emperors hung the votive crowns, fired with the dull light of *cabochon* jewels and enamel plaques. Behind the altar, in the semicircular curve of the apse, were the seven seats of the priests and the throne of the Patriarch, all of gilded silver; while in the curving mosaic vault above them broods from her throne of red, her feet on a green footstool, the Mother of God, her Child held before her, the Archangel Gabriel at her side, blue and white and gold. Truly, as Procopius wrote, *whenever anyone enters the church to pray, he realizes at once that it is not by any human power or skill, but by the influence of God, that it has been built. And so his mind is lifted up to God, and he feels that He cannot be far away, but must love to dwell in this place He has chosen. And this does not happen only to one who sees the church for the first time, but the same thing occurs at each successive visit, as though the sight were each time a new one. No one has ever had enough of this spectacle, but when present in the church men rejoice in what they see, and when they are away from it they love to talk about it.* [19]

Indeed, no description of the wealth and disposition of its various parts can give an impression of the total effect of the church or indicate to what this effect is due. [20] Here, though, is no static architecture, no mere mathematical perfection drained of life and movement. All breaks and flows; the solid masses dissolve and liquefy; do not arrest the eye but persuade it forward and upward through the compelling rhythm of their lines and colours. The walls with their slabs of coloured marble, each with its own pattern of veining, its own tone and shade, seem to be not so much architectural bodies enclosing and dividing as fields of alternating colour, restless strips of smoky blue or dull carnation green or warmer

31

red, without a solid or substantial quality. In the apse and sanctuary whole walls were designed in such sequences of colour intervals, distinguished only from the nave by their darker shades, while in the nave arcades themselves the flat responds hardly possess a structural function: the arches seem to bear only on the columns, leaving the pilasters to act as added elements in the colour-patterns of the walls. Above, the shimmering gold mosaic of vaults and arches, with their flat decorative patterns standing out against the rich gold ground, destroys the effect of weight and seems to merge into a single golden tissue the various areas and sections of the vaulting—an effect made stronger by the diagonal lighting from the windows of the dome and half-domes. The whole lower part of the nave to the springing of the great vaults and arches is one vast field of polychrome activity, the ranges of gleaming columns and the marble revets of the walls seeming to merge into, not to be separate from, the darker intervening spaces of aisles and gallery. Above these warm harmonies of the nave spring the great arches, tympana, half-domes, and dome. Flooded with golden light and floating like weightless spheres, they seem to free themselves from the earth-bound lower portions, hovering in unsubstantial suspense over the dimmer room below. This sense of weightless suspense is, where the main dome itself is concerned, emphasized by the light stream- ing in through the corona of windows above its interior cornice, for this dissolves the bases of the power- ful interior ribs, and the ribs themselves fade out as they rise towards the crown: hence the dome appears to float, held aloft by no external support but by some unseen and inner animation of its own.

Yet this sense of the fluidity of the walls of the nave, of their lack of a substantial architectural char- acter, does not mean that the sense of internal space is also destroyed. But this space seems not to be cut out of the surrounding space of the air and then enclosed by the walls, but to be formed from within and then to be held in place, embraced by the flowing colour-sequences of marble, gold mosaic, and the white pressure of the light breaking in through the windows from the outside. One thinks of a yolk formed within an egg or of a seed within a husk, growing from within, according to some principle of internal generation, rather than simply of an area of space artificially separated off and bound in by the solid structure of the architecture. It is as if the space within the church is a new space, of a quality different from that of the ordinary physical space which surrounds it. Here one touches on the intrinsic significance of the church: of the church as the house of the Divinity. And in this connexion it is to be recalled that this church in particular is the church of the Immortal Wisdom of Christ; that this 'living and acting Logos, the co-essential Son', this 'inseparable Wisdom of the Father', has 'built a material and animated house, that is a temple of his own flesh'[21]; and that as the paradigm of this house which Wisdom has built is the Holy Mother and Virgin Mary, so each visible church, on condition that it con- forms symbolically to this paradigm, perpetuates the role of Mary, and is also the receptacle of the Spirit, its embracing flesh, the material and animated house of the Divine Word: an area of three-dimensional space filled with the presence of the Uncreated Light.

It is for this reason that the physical lighting itself of St. Sophia is not designed merely for aesthetic effect, still less only in order that it may be possible to see or read in the main body of the building. As everything else, it too is subordinate to the overriding spiritual principle out of which the whole church has grown; is intended to convey the sense of the presence of that other Light which it enshrines. Sweep- ing diagonally downwards from the corona of windows in the dome, flooding in from the half-domes and great lunettes, it steeps the central nave in prodigious radiance. Here in this central nave is no dim religious light, none of that mystic emotionalism which lurks in the vibrant gloom of gothic churches, but a supreme effulgence which seems not to derive from any external source but to be self-begotten, born out of its own intrinsic virtue. And this diffusion of light within the nave is graduated upwards: subdued where it meets the shaded twilight which makes its way inwards from the depths of the aisles and galleries; then growing in intensity till it reaches a climax in the corona of the dome, where it again begins to fade, leaving the crown of the dome, the mysterious still point of Light non-manifest, of the God 'who makes the shadows his retreat', in comparative obscurity. The effect again is one of a luminous space in whose alternate zones of light and shade the architectural elements, while still retaining the appearance of their material height and width, weight and support, seem nevertheless to merge and move, flow and blend. The essential architectural forms remain, but seemingly are disburdened of their gravity, transfigured in a disembodied lightness.

Nor at night is the performance of the light any less magnificent, though it is played now by lamp and candle, not by the sun's rays. Again it is Paul the Silentiary who has left a description of its incomparable brilliance: *No word can describe the light at night-time; one might say in truth that some midnight sun illumined the glories of the temple. For the wise forethought of our king has had stretched from the projecting rim of stone, on whose back is firmly planted the temple's air-borne dome, long twisted chains of beaten brass, linked in alternating curves with many windings. And these chains, bending down from every part in a long course, come together as they fall towards the ground. But before they reach the pavement, their path from above is checked, and they finish in unison in a circle. And beneath each chain he has arranged for silver discs to be fitted, hanging circlewise in the air, round the space in the centre of the church. Thus these discs, pendent from their lofty courses, form a coronet above the heads of men. They have been pierced too by the weapon of the skilful workman, in order that they may receive shafts of fire-wrought glass, and hold light on high for men at night.*

And not from discs alone does the light shine at night, but in the circles close by a disc you would see the symbol of the mighty cross, pierced with many holes, and in its pierced back shines a vessel of light. Thus hangs the circling chorus of bright lights. Indeed, you might say that you gazed on the bright constellation of the Heavenly Crown by the Great Bear, and the neighbouring Dragon. Thus through the temple wanders the evening light, brightly shining. In the middle of a larger circle you would find a crown with light-bearing rim; and above in the centre another noble disc spreads its light in the air, so that night is compelled to flee. Near the aisles too, alongside the columns, they have hung in order single lamps apart from one another; and through the whole length of the far-stretching nave is their path. Beneath each they have placed a silver vessel, like a balance pan, and in the centre of this rests a cup of well-burning oil.

There is not however one equal level for all the lamps, for you may see some high, some low, in comely curves of light; and from twisted chains they sweetly flash in their aerial courses, even as shines twin-pointed Hyas fixed in the forehead of Taurus. One might also see ships of silver, bearing a flashing freight of flame, and plying their lofty courses in the liquid air instead of the sea, fearing no gale from south-west, nor from Bootes, sinking late to rest. And above the wide floor you would see shapely beams (with lamps), running between two-horned supports of iron, by whose light the order of priests, bound by the rubrics, perform their duties. Some there are along the floor, where the columns have their bases, and above again others pass, by far-reaching courses, along the crowning work of the walls. Neither is the base of the deep-bosomed dome left without light, for along the projecting stone of the curved cornice the skilful workman suspends single lamps to bronze stakes. As when some handmaid binds round the neck of a royal virgin a graceful chain shining with the glitter of fiery gold, even so has our Emperor fixed round all the cornice a circle of lights, companions everywhere to those below. There is also on the silver columns (of the iconostasis), above their capitals, a narrow way of access for the lamp-lighter, glittering with bright clusters; these one might compare to the mountain-nourished pine, or cypress with fresh branches. From a point ever-widening circles spread down until the last is reached, even that which curves round the base; instead of a root, bowls of silver are placed beneath the trees, with their flaming flowers. And in the centre of this lovely wood, the form of the divine cross, pierced with the prints of the nails, shines with light for mortal eyes.

A thousand others within the temple show their gleaming light, hanging aloft by chains of many windings. Some are placed in the aisles, others in the centre or to east and west, or on the crowning walls, shedding the brightness of flame. Thus the night seems to flout the light of day, and be itself as rosy as the dawn. And whoever gazes on the lighted trees, with their crown of circles, feels his heart warmed with joy; and looking on a boat swathed with fire, or some single lamp, or the symbol of the Divine Christ, all care vanishes from the mind. So with wayfarers through a cloudless night, as they see the stars rising from point to point; one watches sweet Hesperus, another's attention is fixed on Taurus, and a third contemplates Bootes, or Orion and the cold Charles' Wain; the whole heaven, scattered with glittering stars, opens before them, while the night seems to smile on their way.

And he concludes in fitting rhetoric:

Thus through the spaces of the great church come rays of light, expelling clouds of care, and filling the mind with joy. The sacred light cheers all: even the sailor guiding his bark on the waves, leaving behind him the unfriendly billows of the raging Pontus, and winding a sinuous course amidst creeks and rocks, with heart fearful at the dangers of his nightly wanderings—perhaps he has left the Aegean and guides his ship against adverse currents in the Hellespont; awaiting with taut forestay the onslaught of a storm from Africa—does not guide his laden vessel by the light of Cynosure, or the circling Bear, but by the divine light of the church itself. Yet not only does it guide the merchant at night, like the rays from the Pharos on the coast of Africa, but it also shows the way to the living God.

Illustration opposite: Apse of St. Sophia with the mosaic of the Mother of God enthroned, on the vault.

The New Rome

Such, in outline, was the stage; such the décor; and such something of the crowd, wayward and frivolous, solemn and truculent, brilliant and stubborn, that made its way in and out of the shifting scenes of the life of the Byzantine capital. But the drama itself? The complexity of its plot and the roles of its protagonists? The motives of its action? The ideas, supernatural or natural, that it embodied, or failed to embody? Such questions may appear simply rhetorical. We have become so used to looking upon a city merely as a more or less haphazard accumulation of buildings and persons gathered together into one locality in response to economic or social pressures, expressive of no doctrine, ignorant of metaphysics, its inhabitants united by nothing except a common allegiance to their particular self-interests, that the notion that a city may come into being and develop as the organic manifestation of certain coherent and predetermined values is practically inconceivable. Yet cities such as Constantinople are the consequence of precisely such a manifestation. They are not merely administrative or economic capitals of certain more or less well-defined geographical regions, seats of governmental or military power. They are also centres of civilization, centres in which are concentrated and from which radiate the inner 'motive-forces', the dynamic forms, of a particular vision of human life and its destiny.

Nor is this all. For the very notion of 'civilization' itself implies the recognition of something that lies beyond the satisfaction of values of a purely material or even of a purely human nature. Ultimately it is inseparable from the recognition of spiritual values, of values that are superhuman. 'To be civilized' is to have a sense of such values. It is to have a sense of what is sacred. This in its turn means more than that a people, to be civilized, should 'have a religion' relating to the personal conduct of individual life and to the salvation of individual souls, but leaving untouched or relatively untouched the affairs of state—administration, justice, economy, military power, and so on. It also means more than that it should be subject to a government imposed by a religious institution. For a people to be civilized in the fullest sense of the word the ensemble of the life of that people must be dominated by spiritual realities, shot through with the sense of things sacred.

So that a city which, like Constantinople, is the centre of a civilization is one in which the life of its people as a whole is touched and directed by a sense of the sacred, by an allegiance to realities of a superhuman order; whose iconography is evidence of the continual preoccupation of its people with a suprahistoric destiny. To seek to read that iconography, through what records of it still persist, is the task of whoever would understand the inner content of the drama played out on that stage and against that décor of which the city's wall formed both the physical and the symbolic bound.

What image, or what set of images, most strikes the mind's eye where the city of Constantinople is concerned? If one thinks of those panoramas drawn by later travellers which show the city with its Byzantine form still largely intact, pierced though it may be here and there by the tall points of minarets, one thinks perhaps first of all of those great curved shapes breasting the sky—shapes that do indeed seem but condensations of the sky's immensity: the many domes of the city's palaces and churches. And, set over all, seeming to comprehend in its majesty all the multitude of lesser forms that lie below it, is the dome of all Byzantine domes: that of the great church of St. Sophia—a dome so light (to repeat the description by Procopius) that it 'seems not to rest upon solid masonry, but to cover the space beneath as though suspended from heaven by the fabled golden chain'. Procopius here is not speaking simply in a figurative sense; and nor is Paul the Silentiary being merely figurative when he

Illustration opposite: Mosaic in the Narthex of St. Sophia. Constantine the Great presents to the Mother of God the model of his city, and Justinian that of the Cathedral. End of the tenth century.

See the illustrations on pages 101–109.

37

calls the dome of St. Sophia, 'rising into the immeasurable air, the great helmet, which bending over like the radiant heavens embraces the church'. The language is one of an intelligible symbolism; and those who know what the headdress of the Dioscouri signified, and what place those two pagan heroes, gods of the tomb and intermediaries between heaven and earth, had in the Christian imagination of Byzantium, will understand what the poet means when he referred to the dome of St. Sophia as a helmet. For it was a desire to make visible a certain complex of ideas, to expresss in such intelligible symbolism a certain vision of reality, and not any structural and utilitarian interest in a means of covering space that impelled Justinian and the subsequent builders of Byzantium to give such prominence and importance to the dome and to the building of domical churches and palaces; and it was not for nothing that the visitor, approaching the holy city of Constantine from across the dolphin-torn silvery blue of the Sea of Marmara, saw, rising on the spacious platform of the headland, over the masts of the merchant-men and the roofs of the warehouses, over the Hippodrome and the Senate House and the Great Sacred Palace, over the public square of the Augustaeum with its armour-clad statue of the Emperor on his enormous column, the huge domed mass of St. Sophia, at once symbol and embodiment of those motive-forces which gave the city and its life their particular stamp and integrity.

For this church above all others was an expression of that consciousness of a transcendent reality, of a supernatural presence, which lay at the heart of Byzantine life. It was, in terms we have already used,

Byzantine mosaic of a cupola of the Cappella Palatina at Palermo.

the animated house of the Divinity, the living temple of the Logos, replica of heaven upon earth. And of the church, the crowning glory was the dome, invested with a symbolism at once royal and divine. The ancestry of this investiture is a long one and need not be gone into here. It is enough to recall that it was under a dome (though but of a tent) that those divine kings among kings, the Achaemenid kings of Persia who gave the classical world its conception of a divine and universal ruler, used to make their appearance; and that Alexander the Great, in imitation of this, made his appearance, according to Plutarch, in 'a magnificent tent made with fifty gilded posts which carried a sky of rich workmanship'; and that from this derived the jewelled and golden baldachin in which the Byzantine Emperor in his turn made his state appearance. This half-divine, half-royal symbolism was transferred to the dome of the Christian church, and was linked in this elevation with the majesty of Christ, Creator and Pantocrator, the true ruler of heaven and earth. It was his divine presence that animated the space of the dome, so that in this way it became the seat of his celestial authority and compassion, image of the radiant heavens to which man aspired from the darkness in which he lived on earth below. Thus the dome, situated at the central point of the earthly and heavenly kingdom, scene of the manifestation of the Christian Saviour whose image it held, was a symbol and an embodiment both of transcendent power and authority and of that glorious *beyond* and the coming of the Kingdom of God in which the destiny of human life and society was to be fulfilled.

That is why it is no accident that the architectural form of the dome assumes such importance in Byzantium. For the two aspects of its symbolism—the one linked with the idea of royalty and rule, the other with that of the transfiguration and the Second Coming—represented precisely the principal motive-forces that were to determine the development not only of the iconography but also of the whole religious and political structure of the city. They were to give birth to, and be reflected in, what were to become the two dominant forms or images round which the city's life gravitated—forms or images which, however much they might coincide in their divine principle, by no means necessarily harmonized with each other in their historical actualization. These two forms or images are, first, that of the New Rome, with the cult of the Emperor at its centre, and, second, that of the New Jerusalem. And the inner content of the drama of Constantinople was a result of their growth and interplay. But before going on to describe the individual features first of the New Rome and then of the New Jerusalem, something must be said of how their juxtaposition in the historical context of Constantinople came about, and how through this a crucial dichotomy was introduced into the texture of the city's life.

*

The idea that Constantinople should be the New Rome, the new 'ruling city', was implicit in its foundation by Constantine the Great, from the time when, the Sun entering into Sagittarius, with Cancer for horoscope, the neo-Platonist Sopater divined the conjunction of the heavenly bodies as propitious for the happiness and permanence of the new capital about to be dedicated. Like Rome, Constantinople was the 'city of the seven hills'—one of them called 'Capitolium'—and like Rome it was divided into fourteen districts. It had a new Imperial Palace, with the Hippodrome with the Emperor's box next to it, as in Rome. The imperial network of roads started from the 'Milion' on the central square of the Augustaeum, as the *milliarium aureum* stood in the Roman forum. Here, too, was the Senate, as there had been in the old Rome, and here was brought that vast number of statues and other works of ancient art so that the new city should in this respect also be equal to the old. In addition to the name of Constantinopolis, it is said that Constantine also gave the city the mystical pagan name of the old capital, 'Flora' (in its Greek form, 'Anthousa'); while in his forum he set up a statue of the ambivalent Roman Tychê, and struck its copy on the brilliant silver medallions of the mint of Constanti-nople. Summoning from the Eternal City members of its noble families to form the new senatorial class of Constantinople, and housing them in splendid houses, he celebrated, on an issue of local coins, this population of new citizens under the venerable official title of *populus Romanus*. Above all he transferred to the 'second Rome', *altera Roma*, as he liked to call it, the great talisman of the Roman Empire, the Palladium of old Rome, the box, believed to have fallen from the sky, which Aeneas had brought from Troy to the banks of the Tiber; and he immured it at the foot of his statue in the forum. With this identification of the new capital with the status and titles of the old Rome went an acceptance of Rome's whole imperial destiny: that of realizing a universal state under the rule of a single and absolute imperial monarchy. And with this in its turn went the acceptance of the whole symbolic and ritual structure of Rome's universal monarchy.

Here lay the seeds of deep conflict. For Constantine in founding Constantinople under the sign of the Christian Cross had thereby, wittingly or unwittingly, pledged capital and Empire to a new purpose: the manifestation of the triumph of Christianity. Yet at the heart of the Christian faith lay, if not a denial, at least a severe limitation of the imperial destiny itself. 'Render unto Caesar....' Christ had said, meaning that there were whole realms of human thought and action over which the State had no competence; and he had himself set the pattern for Christian behaviour in the face of the State's claim to provide an order within which human life could be perfected by his triumphal entry into Jerusalem, an entry whose climax was the Cross with its unmistakable repudiation of a this-worldly Messiahship: in the hostile terrestrial city he had perfected the loyalty tested in the wilderness temptations and sustained with patient devotion all the way from Galilee to Gethsemane. The State is not the Kingdom, the will of God could not be consummated through the authority of its rulers and custodians: it was to this under-standing that the Christians of the first centuries remained faithful. Christianity spread for three centuries, not with an Empire, but in spite of one, not in conquest but in catacombs.

This did not mean that Christians were resolutely and uncompromisingly hostile to the Empire. If God's purpose for man could not be fulfilled within or by the State, this did not signify that the State and its ministers played no part in God's providence. On the contrary, they played a most legitimate part, one which a St. Paul, for instance, was able to recognize and proclaim in categorical terms: *Let every soul be subject unto the higher powers. For there is no power but of God: the powers that be are ordained of God. Whosoever therefore resisteth the power, resisteth the ordinance of God; and they that resist shall receive to them-selves damnation. For rulers are not a terror to good works, but to the evil. Wilt thou then not be afraid of the power? Do that which is good and thou shalt have praise of the same: For he is the minister of God to thee for good. But if thou do that which is evil, be afraid; for he beareth not the sword in vain: for he is the minister of God, a revenger to execute wrath upon him that doeth evil.* [22] It was not to denying to Caesar his throne that Christians of the first three centuries devoted their energies; far from this being the case, they were, in things lawful and honest, readily obedient to the imperial, civil power, even though that power might be identified with such figures as Nero or Domitian; and even when confronted by the choice of insurrection or suffering, they consistently chose the second. They were in the State as followers of a new Gospel, not against it as supporters of a new Caesar. But it was precisely as followers of the new Gospel, not as citizens of the Empire, that they were bound by the most absolute loyalties; and if they did not deny to Caesar his throne, they were not on that account ready to recognize this throne as that of God, or its occupant as divine. *What man is more concerned about the Emperor than we are?* asked one of the leaders of a Christian community around the year A.D. 250. *Who loves him more honestly than we? For we pray incessantly for him that he may be granted long life and that he may rule the nations with a just sword and know an age of peace and plenty in his Empire. Then we pray for the welfare of the army and for the blessing of*

mankind and of the world. But we cannot sacrifice to the Emperor in the temple. For who may pay divine honours to a man of flesh and blood? Here was a clear breach, one that no apology could heal, with the Roman imperial claim: the claim of an Aurelian to be born Lord and God *(deus et dominus natus)* or of a Domitian to a similar status; the claim of the absolute divine authority of the Roman monarchy. And Christians are committed to a defiance of this authority in any state demands that flout the rights and claims of God as revealed in his and their Gospel.

Constantine the Great had recognized this breach when, defying the whole authority of Graeco-Roman antiquity and the classical religion of the State, he separated the spiritual side of life from political and state control. But he did not on that account surrender his quasi-divine status as the Roman Emperor nor what was implicit in this, a conception of the god-like Empire, with its corresponding mystical and symbolic structure of relationships between heaven and earth, the divine and the human, the invisible and the visible. Thus was posed the problem of how this status and conception and structure, all of which had their issue in the general theory that the political order could of itself constitute a divine society—how could this be reconciled with a religion, now in the way of becoming the 'official' religion of the State, whose Founder had explicitly rejected all this-worldly status and authority and whose divine society was that heavenly Jerusalem, the citizenship of which could only be conferred on those who through the Way of the Gospel had overcome the world and its politics?

Of the Christian apologists for the Constantinian settlement who sought to resolve this problem the most persuasive and influential was undoubtedly Eusebius, bishop of Caesarea (c. 265–340). For him the status of the Emperor and the Empire was the direct consequence of his reading of the Christian tradition. The roots of Christianity, according to this reading, went back behind the actual historical incarnation of Christ himself to the pre-Mosaic era of the patriarchs. The patriarchs had 'a free and unfettered mode of religion, being regulated by the manner of life which is in accordance with nature, so that they had no need of laws to rule them'. From this primordial purity of the faith of the patriarchs Mosaic Judaism was a deviation and a falling off, one which had to be repaired by the incarnation of Christ, who, fulfilling the Law of Moses, restored the ancient and original dispensation. Christ 'mended that most ancient and primitive breach' which had been made in the working of God's purpose by the emergence of Judaism, and the religion which he preached to all the nations was the ancient universal faith of the pre-Mosaic world. The Mosaic dispensation was a local and temporary affair and applied only to the Jews and in particular to the Jews of Palestine: their lapse into idolatry had called forth this lower and less perfect way as a means through which they might be re-educated; and the destruction of the Temple by the Romans signified that its end had now come. [23]

The Christians were therefore the new patriarchs, consecrated to fulfilling the divine purpose which had been interrupted by the Jewish deviation. The main course of this fulfilment was implicit in that focal point of the patriarchal era, God's threefold promise to Abraham: that his descendants should be numberless; that they should possess a common territory; and that they should be a source of blessing to mankind. This promise had been made to Abraham; but the election of the individual extends to that of the nation sprung from him: such a nation should be a chosen nation, its people a chosen people. The conception of such a human society, of a people chosen under God, dedicated to his service and pledged to a corporate salvation—a conception adopted by the Christians from the Jews—is therefore implicit in God's promise to Abraham; and its fulfilment must be a theocracy of all mankind in which God rules over his people.

This theocracy had not been realized in the patriarchal era. It had not been realized, though it had been prepared and prefigured, in the Roman Empire which at the time of Christ's birth into the world had, by divine providence, united all people under one rule. But what had been proposed to the patriarchs, and

43

partially implemented under the Pax Romana, was to be fulfilled by Constantine. The new *imperium* of Constantine was of divine origin; was founded not only upon the tradition of Augustus, but also upon that of Abraham and Christ; and the Promise which Christians in the first three centuries after Christ had striven to fulfil in spite of the Empire was now to be realized by means of the Empire. The Empire was to be a worldly instrument in the hand of God for the realization of his purpose; and Constantine had been elected by God to achieve the corporate salvation of his chosen people in this new Christian theocracy: 'Our Emperor', writes Eusebius, 'derives the source of his authority from above, and is strong in the power of his sacred title. Bringing those whom he rules on earth to the only-begotten Logos or Saviour, he renders them fit subjects for His Kingdom.' [24] If the end of individual human life is now envisaged as a participation in the extra-temporal and divine life of the resurrected Saviour, then its counterpart where the temporal ordering of human society as a whole is concerned is the submission of all people to Christianity.

It was in such a form as this that the imperial idea, with its focal point in the principle of a universal monarchy, was accommodated to the Christian dispensation; and it was the acceptance of this form on the part of Emperor and people, and their desire to embody it, that explains how the whole symbolic and ritual structure of the divine kingship, transferred from Rome to Constantinople by Constantine the Great, persisted in the latter city alongside, if not always in harmony with, the symbolic and ritual structure of the New Jerusalem. What did this idea of divine kingship amount to in Byzantium, and how was it embodied in the ritual and symbolic structure of the Emperor's and the city's life?

Emblem from the sarcophagus of
Constantine the Great.

The idea of royalty which lay at the heart of the conception of a theocratic society, whether in Christian or non-Christian form, was inherent in the theory that the human and terrestrial order must be modelled on the divine order. As God is in his Heaven, so must the king—the *basileus*—be in his City, the image of Heaven; as the Deity is the regulator of the cosmic order, the invariable centre round which all revolves, so must the *basileus* be the regulator of the social order, the invariable centre round which all human affairs revolve. This imitation of the divine by the human order is not regarded as abstract or mechanical, in the sense that the two orders are mutually self-contained and without any interrelation. Rather the *basileus* himself is regarded as providing a link, a bridge between them. The *basileus* is a symbol of the cosmic king, the hieratic figure in whom is embodied a mythical or mystic sense of the incorporation of a ray of the divine Logos, Heaven's King. In this way a link is established between the head of the social organization and the divine principle of the religion on which it depends, between (in the case of Byzantium) the *basileus* and Christ. The *basileus* is the channel through which a spiritual influence flows into the social order, he is a kind of coincidence of the terrestrial and celestial poles, to such an extent that in a certain sense it appears that he transcends the normal distinction between the sacerdotal and the temporal powers. This is the basic significance of a theocratic monarchy, and it is not to be confused with the type of monarchy dominated by a religious organization on the lines of those kingships that the medieval papacy sought to establish in the Latin West. The *basileus* is not a divine incarnation, but the elect of God, a living image of the incarnation, an always actual event which the person of the *basileus* makes sensible for the people. This is the proper and only real meaning of the royal idea.

The ramifications of this are considerable. The modern mentality, its sense of things sacred deadened, divides the affairs of state—administration, justice, economy, military power—from religion, and, where it recognizes the latter at all, relates it more or less exclusively to the personal conduct of life and the salvation of souls. The idea of society as a religious organism has been eliminated, and with it all question of a theocracy: there is no 'God', and the business of government is the satisfaction merely of material needs which can be met by improved technological methods. This was not the case where Byzantium was concerned. Far from dividing the affairs of state and of society in general from religion, both were saturated by religion. Religion, it must be repeated, was not simply an aspect of Byzantine life; it was the element within which that life moved and had its being. The keys of this religion were in the hands of the saints and the sacred hierarchy. But the dramatic representation of the inner sense of its myth was centred in the *basileus*. Hence all actions of the *basileus*, as well as the means through which they are implemented, have a sacred and symbolic significance; and his life is regulated by rites through which the type of the God-man is represented in all its aspects and in every circumstance. It is for this reason that what the *basileus* is as a human individual is a secondary matter—a matter of his own private salvation—though, as we shall see, the distinction between a worthy and an unworthy Emperor may always be recognized. But in the daily ritual of the court it is the *basileus* as the incarnation of the sacred principle of royalty who officiates: not the historical person but his purely hieratic-symbolic aspect. It is to this aspect that everything connected with him is consecrated: his throne, his crown, his palace, his court, his vestments, his public appearances, his statues, his images, the mystical procession of his days, his whole palatine and imperial service, his laws, and everything else related to his office.

All this is not to say that Christianity had in no way modified the imperial idea in its classical Roman form. It had modified it, and in many ways. First of all, the linear conception of time which in Christianity takes precedence over (and virtually replaces) the cyclic conception of time of the 'classical' religions had added a historical perspective, a sense of the unfolding of the divine purpose in and through time, to the static theory of imitation ($\mu\acute{\iota}\mu\eta\sigma\iota\varsigma$)—the imperial order being a static copy of God's order in Heaven—on which Roman autocratic rule had been based. Secondly, the absolutism of the Emperor itself was considerably attenuated. It is true that the Emperor's office and power were regarded as deriving from divine authority; but the Emperor was not regarded as himself a god, nor was the religion which he was chosen to support and spread a state religion: both Christ himself and the interpreters of the Christian tradition had already directly indicated that the authority of Caesar did not extend to matters of faith and dogma, and Eusebius, the great apologist for the imperial idea in its Christian form, is further clarifying this limitation when he says that the Emperor is ordained 'to overlook whatever is external to the Church'.[25] For the corollary to holding the office of Christian Emperor is the Emperor's responsibility to the divine law; and the task of determining this law lay not with the Emperor but with the apostolic ministers of the Christian Church. The Emperor, as a Christian, was a member, and not the head, of the *ecclesia*, and as such he was subject to its discipline. 'If the *basileus*', wrote a tenth-century Patriarch, Nicholas the Mystic, 'inspired by the devil, gives an order contrary to the divine law, no one need obey him.... Every subject may rise against every administrative act contrary to the law and even against the Emperor, if he is dominated by his passions.' It is easy to point to frequent instances in

Byzantine history in which the prelates themselves ignored this prescription; and it is easy also to point to occasions on which the Emperor has seemed to interfere directly in the interior life of the Church. But in spite of this the ecclesiastical hierarchy preserved through a period of more than a thousand years the fundamental doctrines proclaimed in the fourth and fifth centuries by the Fathers of the Church on the subject of the relationship between Church and State: that the Emperor as the temporal power is subservient to laws higher than his own; that his authority is limited by that of the Church he serves; that if he is a heretic he must be condemned; that if he is orthodox he is still in need of salvation. And correspondingly it may be said that throughout this same long period, no Emperor—neither Justinian, nor members of the Heraclian dynasty, nor the Iconoclast Emperors—ever succeeded in imposing permanently a dogma contrary to the Orthodox Christian tradition. Of the tenacity with which both clergy and people held to this tradition there could perhaps be no more moving demonstration than the spectacle which took place towards the end of this long period and at a time when an alliance with the Latin West seemed clearly to be the only alternative to the destruction of the Empire at the hands of the Turks—the spectacle of the greater part of the clergy and the congregation of the people of the imperial capital deserting their great church, St. Sophia, where the last crowned *basileus* had come to proclaim, in defiance of Orthodox doctrine, the end of the schism and union with Rome.

But with these essential modifications, the dramatic representation of the myth of the universal theocracy, centred in the hieratic-symbolic presence of the consecrated *basileus*, was enacted at Constantinople for more than a thousand years. The various scenes of this divine-human drama in which the *basileus*, under the sign of the Cross, was the protagonist, are described in several documents, chief of which is the vast manual of imperial ceremonial, the *De Ceremoniis*, compiled by the Emperor Constantine VII Porphyrogenitus (913–959). From these may be reconstructed the course of that ceaseless palatine liturgy, from the birth of the new prince in the porphyry pavilion at the water's edge; through the coronation and marriage; through the everyday ritual dictated by the religious calendar, the investitures, audiences, banquets, festivities, the triumphs, the sessions of the Hippodrome, the religious processions; to the last ceremony of entombment at the church of the Holy Apostles: all these separate scenes of the drama in which legend, allegory, dogma, and knowledge crystallized in the service of the great symbol of corporate human salvation, set in the loveliest setting man and nature could devise, the city itself, where the citizen, even while acting his normal role, goldsmith or silk-weaver, tanner or baker, was yet elevated above himself and held in creative tension by his sense of participating in the cosmic vision which the ceremony set forth.

*

The young prince of the imperial house of Byzantium was from his earliest years surrounded with ceremonial. On the announcement of his birth, the Patriarch, with a company of metropolitans and archbishops, arrived at the Palace and said a prayer for the child 'born in the purple'. Then the Emperor received the high dignitaries of the Senate, who congratulated him and presented their good wishes. Five days after the birth, the people of Constantinople gathered, at the order of the *basileus*, in the Hippodrome, and acclaimed the Emperor and the Empress, and saluted the new-born prince with his name. After a further three days, the child was carried to the entrance of the church and, after a prayer had been said and he had been clothed in white, he was given his name. Then, in recollection of the Magi, wives and widows of high-ranking dignitaries brought presents and saluted the Empress on her happy deliverance. After them, the dignitaries themselves were introduced, bowing before the cradle and paying their respects to the sovereign mother. Meanwhile, the city was granted a seven-day period of rejoicing. A special spiced beverage was prepared for drinking to the Empress' health, and this was issued freely in court and public square alike.

The next major ceremonial function was the baptism. This in the case of an imperial prince took place only after a period of religious instruction, and was performed in a public church, the great baptistery of St. Sophia. Now the whole city was decorated with gold-embroidered silks and messages of good-will poured in from everywhere. After the ceremony, the baptized child was conducted back to the Palace in great pomp. All wore snow-white vestments, the patricians and dignitaries carried lighted candles, the Emperor, clothed in purple, walked by the child, while the Empress waited at the Palace to receive them. 'If terrestrial and perishable things are of such splendour', exclaimed a witness of one such spectacle, 'what will be the splendour of heavenly things, that no eye has seen, and no ear has heard, and that has never entered the heart of man?'

But it was only after he had taken his place on the throne that the royal prince entered fully into the complex labyrinth of palatine and imperial ritual. This could only officially be after his coronation. Until this had been performed, and the crown had been placed on his head by the Patriarch, the Emperor was not 'legitimate'. Here may be noted something of the modification of the Roman imperial idea which had been brought about by Christianity, as well as something of the extremely complex interrelationship between Church and State in the Christian Empire. Originally the divine mandate to which the Emperor owed his providential election was indicated in the consent of the Senate, the army, and the people of Constantinople to his assumption of the imperial office. But with time the Senate, though it continued to exist in name, lost all effective power, while the people's role in the Emperor's election was reduced to one of formal acclamation only. Acclamation by the army remained a political reality, for no ruler could have kept himself on the throne without the support of the army. But what did become an act essential for full investiture was the religious coronation ceremony performed by the Patriarch. Yet the office of the Patriarch, bishop of Constantinople and most senior of the Eastern bishops, was, in spite of its ecclesiastical character, itself very much at the discretion of the Emperor. It was in the first place in order to raise the dignity of the imperial capital that, as the third canon of the Council of Constantinople (381) declared, the bishop of Constantinople was given a degree of honour second only to the bishop of Old Rome on the Tiber, 'because the city of which he is bishop is the New Rome'; and it was for the same reason that seventy-five years later, at the Council of Chalcedon, the bishop of Constantinople was accorded 'equal prerogatives' with the bishop of Old Rome. Then, though the election of the Patriarch was nominally in the hands of the metropolitans, the reality of elective power was often with the Emperor, who chose the Patriarch from a list of three names presented to him by the ecclesiastical authorities, and even on occasions imposed his own candidate—just as on occasions he arrogated the right to depose him, with or without ecclesiastical consent. There is of course a certain logic in the fact that the Emperor played this important part in the election of the Patriarch: the Empire was a Christian Empire, and thus the well-being and continuity of the Empire depended to a certain extent if not entirely upon the well-being of the ecclesiastical hierarchy, of which the Patriarch was the senior member. At the same time, the Patriarch was no mere creature of the Emperor, as, indeed, we have already seen. For first of all, in theory at least he owed his appointment to God, and only to the Emperor as God's instrument: 'The Holy Trinity, through the intermediary of the imperial majesty with which it has invested me, names you...': so ran the formula of the Patriarch's investiture; and this implied an independence of the Emperor. And secondly, while in the Latin West there was a tendency, especially in the later medieval period, to reduce the authority of metropolitans, archbishops, and bishops, in relationship to that of the Popes, in the Greek East this authority was preserved *vis-à-vis* both the Patriarch and the Emperor; and it was in the continued independence of this authority that the guarantee of the Emperor's submission to the divine law as expressed through the Church ultimately lay.

So the Emperor's coronation by the Patriarch had far more than a token reality: it was the visible confirmation of God's choice and the visible expression of the Emperor's acceptance of his role as God's servant in his terrestrial rule: *I, ..., in Christ God faithful Emperor and autocrat of the Romans,* ran the oath which the intending *basileus* had to submit to the Patriarch before his coronation, *I put forth with my own hand that I believe in one God, the Father almighty, maker of heaven and earth, and of all things visible and invisible* (and he repeats the words of the Creed). *Further I accept and confess and confirm the apostolic and divine traditions, the ordinances and definitions of the seven oecumenical councils and the local synods convened from time to time, and the privileges and customs of the most holy great Church of God. In addition I confirm and accept all doctrines that our most holy fathers here or elsewhere decreed and declared rightly and canonically and irreproachably. Likewise I promise to abide and perpetually prove myself a faithful and true servant and son of the holy Church, to be gracious and kind to my subjects as is reasonable and fitting, to refrain from infliction of death and mutilation and anything resembling these in so far as it is possible, and to submit to all truth and justice. Furthermore all things which the holy fathers rejected and anathematized, I also reject and anathematize, and I believe with my whole mind and soul and heart the aforesaid holy creed. All these things I promise to keep before the holy catholic and apostolic Church of God. On the... day of... in year—I, ..., in Christ God faithful Emperor and autocrat of the Romans, having submitted it with my own hand, deliver this to my most holy lord and oecumenical Patriarch, lord..., and with him to the divine and sacred synod.*

The actual ceremony of the coronation which might now take place had two phases: the first, which seems to have been dispensed with on certain occasions and which anyhow was of decreasing importance, was that in which the Emperor was elevated, Roman-wise, upon a shield in the public square of the Augustaeum; while the second was the religious ceremony proper, which took place in St. Sophia and was presided over by the Patriarch. A Russian pilgrim visiting the city in 1391 has left an account, differing but little from earlier accounts, of the religious phase of the ceremony:

In the year 6899, the eleventh day of February, the Sunday of the Prodigal Son, His Holiness the Patriarch Antony crowned the Emperor Manuel and the Empress. And this is how the coronation took place. During the whole of the preceding night a vigil was held in St. Sophia. Early in the morning I too went there and there were many people present: men in the main body of the church and women in the galleries. It is very cleverly arranged: all the women are behind silk curtains and no one is able to see the ornaments of their faces, while they can see everything.

The cantors stood, magnificently dressed: their chasubles were as long and wide as their surplices and they all wore a girdle; as for the sleeves of their chasubles, they were broad and long, some of damask, others of silk with epaulettes ornamented with gold, pearls, and lace. They wore a pointed headdress ornamented with lace, and there were many of them. They were so well organized that they might have been painted. Their leader was a most handsome man; his locks were white as snow.

Romans and Spaniards were there, Franks from Galata, Byzantines and Genoese, Venetians and Hungarians, and they were splendid to look at. They stood on either side; the costumes of some were of purple velvet, while those of others were of cherry-coloured velvet. Their arms were embroidered on their chests and many of them were decorated with pearls....

To the right, beneath the galleries, was a platform about twelve feet high and fourteen feet long, all covered with purple on which two golden thrones had been placed.

The Emperor had passed the whole night in the galleries; and, at the first hour of day, he came down from the galleries and entered the holy church by the great front entrance-door, called the imperial door. During this time, the cantors intoned a most beautiful and astonishing chant, surpassing understanding. The imperial cortège advanced so slowly that it took three hours from the great door to the platform bearing the throne. Twelve men-at-arms, covered with mail from head to foot, surrounded the Emperor. Before him marched two standard-bearers with black hair: the poles of their standards, their costume, and their headdress were red. Before these standard-bearers went heralds: their rods were plated with silver....

Ascending the platform, the Emperor put on the imperial purple and the imperial diadem and the crenated crown. And coming down from the platform, he went up (to the galleries), and then came back with the Empress, and they sat down on the golden thrones.

Then the holy liturgy began. And the Emperor and the Empress were seated on their golden thrones. And before the Great Entry, two archdeacons approached the Emperor and made him a slight bow. Getting up, the Emperor went towards the sanctuary, the standard-bearers before him and the men-at-arms about him. Once the Emperor was in the sanctuary, the standard-bearers and the men-at-arms ranged themselves in front of the sanctuary on either side of the royal door. The Emperor was clothed in a short purple chasuble reaching down to the girdle. And at the Great Entrance, the Emperor walked carrying a candle, while the Patriarch remained standing in the centre of the church. Then, during the procession, the Patriarch, accompanied by the Emperor, ascended the ambo. Then the crown of the Emperor and that of the Empress were brought to the Patriarch on a platter, both of them covered. Two archdeacons made a slight bow to the Empress, and she approached the ambo. And the Patriarch placed a cross round the Emperor's neck and a cross in his hand, and, taking the imperial crown, the Patriarch blessed the Emperor and placed the crown on his head; and putting the other crown in his hand he commanded him to descend and to place it on the head of the Empress. Then, from below, the Emperor saluted the Patriarch with his hand and with the crown, and the Patriarch, standing on the ambo, blessed the Emperor and the Empress from above, and both of them together bowed to him.

Then they returned to their places and sat themselves on the thrones; and the Patriarch made his entry into the sanctuary by the royal door and continued the divine service. When the Cherubic hymn was chanted, the archdeacons again approached the Emperor and bowed to him as before. And the Emperor got up and entered the sanctuary where he was again clothed in the chasuble. The Emperor walked in front of the holy sacraments (during the Great Entry), a lighted candle in hand.

Who can describe the beauty of all this?

The procession of the holy sacraments lasted as long as the Cherubic hymn. And when the holy sacraments re-entered the sanctuary, the Emperor censed the altar.

The Emperor stayed at the altar till the time of holy communion. And when the time for holy communion came, the archdeacons went and bowed before the Empress. When the Empress had descended from the throne, the people present tore the hangings of the throne and each tried to grab a piece. And the Empress entered by the southern door into the aisle of the altar and there she received holy communion. As for the Emperor, he communicated with the clergy from the hands of the Patriarch at the altar of Christ. Then the Emperor came out of the sanctuary, and the

Patriarch, descending from the patriarchal throne, also came out; and the Emperor approached him clothed in the purple mantle and with the crown on his head; the Patriarch gave his blessing, as he did also to the Empress, and he charged him to preserve the Orthodox faith without alteration, and not to change the ancient laws, or to take what was not his due, but to fear God above all and to remember death: 'For you are dust and to dust you will return', and so on, as it is laid down in the statutes. And after the Patriarch's word, no one was able or dared to approach the Emperor in order to felicitate him, neither princes nor boyars nor soldiers. But he was at once approached by marble-cutters and tomb-makers who had come to bring him samples of marble and stone of various sorts and to ask him: 'What shall be the aspect of the tomb Your Majesty shall order?', reminding him in this way that man is mortal and perishable, that he is only in passage in this vain and poor life that flows by and disappears so quickly. 'Have care for your soul and direct the affairs of your Empire piously; be as humble as you are exalted; for the exalted are more severely tested, and the proud, in their pride, sin before God as much as blasphemers; fear the Lord always and be humble, good, and compassionate; and heavenly love and the grace of the Lord will preserve and save you.' They spoke to him in this way as it is written in the ordinances; then the princes, the strategoi, the priests, the soldiers, and all the nobles said to him the words customarily said on these occasions. And after the coronation, having received the blessing of the Patriarch, the Emperor went out of the church with great humility, and meekness, and fear of God, and coins of gold were showered on him which the people grabbed with both hands.

Such is the ancient tradition according to which the Emperor is crowned. And it was thus that the Emperor Manuel was crowned by the Patriarch Antony and by all the holy clergy, according to ancient traditions.[26]

Though coronation was an essential part of the Emperor's investiture with the full dignity of his office, it was by no means a rite reserved exclusively for hereditary princes of the line 'born in the purple'. There was indeed no law regulating succession, and though legitimate dynastic primogeniture and masculinity conferred strong claims on a candidate, and especially from the eleventh century onwards, the whole theory of the monarchy left the door open for intervention.[27] For by whatever means he reached the throne, the Emperor's election was always in fact due to precisely such an intervention: to the direct choice of God; and by however many formalities and safeguards he might surround himself, his continued occupation of his office was due entirely to God's continuing support and inspiration. And what God gave, God could take away. So that although an Emperor has received a divine mandate to rule, and may legitimately seek to transmit that mandate to his dynastic successor, his power is not his through any virtue of his own, but only by the grace of God; and should God 'repent' of his choice, should the Emperor or his dynastic successors err from the divine path, degenerate, or fail, this grace may at any moment be withdrawn. In such a case a further intervention is called forth, which may if necessary take a violent form. The divine right of the Emperor depended after all on his office, not on his person; and if the person sought to abuse the office he was violating what was not his to abuse and what might on that account be taken from him. For the Emperor as a person, as an individual and not in his hieratic-symbolic capacity, was fallible, could transgress the divine will. If the error was slight, it might be pardoned; if it was serious, it might kindle the divine wrath. And this wrath could be expressed in many and unpredictable ways; could be slow to fall, or could fall like lightning; could be sharp or sparing. But it was always irrevocable.

This meant that the theory of the divine right of the imperial office was double-edged where the individual Emperor was concerned: if his occupation of the throne was due to no human agency but solely to divine decree and protection, and was, therefore, given that decree and protection, infallible, he personally had no guarantee of God's continuing solicitude: he could not bind the Spirit. Indeed, in a certain sense the only clear indication that he still enjoyed divine support and favour was the fact that he still occupied the imperial throne. Should he be removed therefrom, by assassination, fear, old age,

The Emperor Nicephorus Botoniates and the Empress Mary crowned by Christ. Miniature from a MS. of the Homilies of St. John Chrysostom; about 1078. Bibliothèque Nationale, Paris.

patrician pressure, or by any other means, this was an equally clear sign that the mandate of his power had been withdrawn, that he no longer enjoyed divine support and favour, no longer had any claim to the throne of which he had once been the possessor. Hence the endless plots and counterplots: in practice it often seemed that the only way of telling the state of the divine will was by putting it to the test, and should an attempt on the throne be successful then it could be regarded as a legitimate expression of God's wrath, as the execution of divine judgement on one from whom God's protecting inspiration had been withdrawn.

53

It is this ambivalence surrounding the chief imperial office—the double-edged authority of the *fait accompli*—that explains much in the lives and fortunes of individual Emperors which would otherwise be attributed to arbitrary caprice or to solemn hypocrisy, rather than to the innate logic of the position. It explains a certain fatalism that seems often to govern an Emperor's course of action when he feels power slipping from him, a tendency not to resist or to oppose but to surrender to whoever has the strength to dispossess him: 'It is God, that much is certain, who elevated me to the throne', said the Empress Irene (797–802) to Nicephorus I, who had deposed her, 'and I attribute my fall to my own sins. May God's name be blessed, however it is. I ascribe to God your elevation to the Empire, for nothing can happen except by his will. It is by God that Emperors reign. I consider you as the elect of God, and I prostrate myself before you as before an Emperor'; and she retired in her exile to a convent. It explains too what might appear to be a lack of loyalty among the nobility, the army, and the people to a deposed Emperor, the readiness with which they accept a usurpation, violent or peaceful, and with which they recognize the usurper's legitimacy: to continue in loyalty towards someone who by the fact that he has been dispossessed of the throne reveals that he no longer enjoys God's favour would be a kind of sacrilege, as it would also be a kind of sacrilege to withhold recognition from someone who by the fact of his successful raid on the throne has demonstrated his divine election. And it must be remembered in this connexion that the high officers of state, the chiefs of the army, and all other imperial dignitaries were appointed by the Emperor in his capacity as God's delegate, and thus they held their offices, as the Emperor held his office, by divine right, and this even if they had bought their offices, as they often did; and their loyalty was therefore to God, and to God's elect, not to the individual person of the Emperor who had invested them. To continue to serve an Emperor from whom the divine mandate had clearly been withdrawn was not only stupid; it was also to oppose providence. It explains further, this ambivalence, the persistent efforts on the part of the reigning monarchs to scrutinize the divine will, to read the 'signs' of God's favour or disfavour—efforts which often led the Emperors into the forbidden practice of magic and divination (*sileat omnibus perpetuo divinendi curiositas*, read Justinian's Code, which in this instance the Emperors themselves were frequently the first to break). And it is this finally that explains the extreme violence and often brutality with which an intending usurper often acted; for if the reigning *basileus* continued to occupy the throne after the divine mandate had in fact been withdrawn, he was himself then the most monstrous usurper, usurping what was in a sense the throne of God itself; while the attacker was either an instrument of God's wrath, in itself sufficient justification for any act, whatever its character, or, inspired by the devil, was striking against God's lawful representative, a crime for which the worst punishment was inadequate. Hence, whatever the circumstances, the protagonist in an attack on the throne was caught in the extremes of tension, and his actions correspondingly might bear the signs of this: it is no accident that of the eighty-eight Emperors reigning from 323 to 1453, from Constantine I to Constantine XI (not including co-Emperors, who did not exercise full powers), thirty died a violent death, in one way or another (strangulation, poisoning, under torture, and so on), while another thirteen took refuge, temporarily or for the rest of their lives, in a monastery.

Many of these violent deaths did in fact have a most macabre character: that, in 610, of Phocas, for instance, who, stripped of the purple and dressed in a heavy black tunic, was brought before his dispossessor, Heraclius, and who, replying to the latter's question, 'Wretch, is this how you have ruled the Empire?' with the words, 'Rule it better yourself', was hurled to the ground; shorn of hands, feet, private parts, and head; paraded, thus dismembered, on pikes round the city, and finally burnt. Or that, on 26 December 820, of Leo V the Armenian: his assassins, robed as priests, had entered the palatine chapel in the early hours of the morning with the priests who were to celebrate matins, at which the Emperor, who prided himself on his voice, was always present. Hidden in the obscurity of the church,

The Emperor John VI
Cantacuzenus, as
Emperor and as monk.
Miniature in a MS. of
the Emperor's
theological works,
produced about 1370
in Constantinople.
Bibliothèque
Nationale, Paris.

they awaited the signal. This the Emperor himself was to give: as he chanted the hymn: 'They despise everything out of love for the Almighty', they sprang forward. But, the morning being cold, clerics and *basileus* had their heads covered, and the assassins mistook the identity of their victim. By the time they realized their error, Leo had leapt on to the altar where, seizing the censer (or the cross, according to other accounts), he sought to defend himself. In vain: he was overcome, his head was cut off, and his body was dragged into the Hippodrome. There it was cut into pieces and put into a sack which was then thrown into the same boat as that in which his wife, the Empress, and their four sons were to be transported to an island in the Sea of Marmara. Or that, thirdly, on the night of 11 December 969, of Nicephoros II Phocas. The old ascetic general, conqueror of the Saracens, was lying asleep in the bed-chamber of his sea-shore palace, not on the imperial couch, but as usual on a tiger-skin on the floor, wrapped in the mantle of one of his former spiritual advisers, now dead, the monk Michael Maleinos. Admitted by his wife, the amorous Theophano, the assassins entered and, while he called on the Mother of God for help, beat and stabbed him to death. Decapitated, his body was pitched out of the window into the snow; his head, held up by its long hair and lit by torches, was dangled before the terrified crowd; while his supplanter, his former comrade-in-arms Tzimisces, donned the scarlet imperial buskins and the other insignia of office and sat himself on the royal throne in the splendid Chrysotriclinos, acclaimed by conspirators and partisans as the new Emperor. Or that, finally and most gruesome of all, in 1185, of Andronicus I Comnenus, who, having been chained for days in a pillory, beaten black and blue, had his teeth broken with hammers and one hand cut off, was tied, naked and half dead, to the back of a sick, scraggy camel, his head beneath the animal's tail, and was thus paraded through the streets of the city. A girl threw boiling water in his face, someone plucked out an eye. After this he was strung up for torture in the Hippodrome, where finally, still alive, still repeating over and over, 'Lord, have mercy on me. Why do you still strike a broken reed?', he was put out of his misery by a sword plunged into his entrails. As he died, the bleeding stump of his arm swung up to his mouth: 'Look', was the comment, 'he can't feed himself any longer on the blood of the people, so he's sucking his own blood.' It goes without saying that the punishment of those who failed in their attempts on the life or throne of the Emperor—and there were many who so failed—was equally terrible. But both the excesses of the attack and of the punishment if it failed lay in the inexorable logic of the imperial system.

Thus it was by no means always the law of primogeniture that determined the imperial succession. Indeed, many Emperors, examples such as those given above before them, were reluctant to commit their sons in advance to such a destiny, and would at least demand a solemn vow of recognition from the people before they did so. Not that this either was necessarily binding—how, given the logic of the system, could it be binding? Supplicated by the Senate, army, and people to associate his son Constantine with the throne, Leo IV the Khazar (775–780) hesitated: 'He is my only son', he said, 'and I am afraid that should I elevate him to the throne you will put him to death, after my decease, in order to take another master.' So he demanded from the Senate, the army, and the people a solemn vow sworn on the Cross that they would never recognize Emperors other than his sons and their descendants. The formula of the oath was laid on the altars of churches, and the coronation of the heir apparent was celebrated amid great pomp. 'I give you my son as Emperor', Leo added, 'but take note that it is from Christ's own hands that you receive him.' And the assembled crowd cried in answer: 'Be it sworn, Son of God, that it is from your hand that we receive as Emperor the Master Constantine and we swear to serve him faithfully and to die for him.' In spite of such precaution, Constantine VI was the object of successive plots and was finally dethroned and blinded by his own mother with the complicity of the Senate. Similarly, in 842 the Emperor Theophilus, on his death-bed, made the Senate swear allegiance to his son. But this son, Michael III, was assassinated and the Senate immediately proclaimed his murderer, Basil I, as Emperor. Similarly, too, Leo VI (886–912) received the Senate's oath of loyalty to his son, the future Constantine VII Porphyrogenitus. But Constantine yielded effective rule without opposition to Romanus I Lecapenus. If God gave the power to govern, he could equally well take it away, and no human oath could in any way affect his decision.

By whatever means the Emperor reached the throne, once he was consecrated in his office his life was subject to intense ritual prescription. The centre of this was the Sacred Palace itself, a solar temple, or a 'Holy Land' at the heart of the universe, where the throne was the throne of God. For symbolically (and it is to a universal symbolism that we here refer) the Sacred Palace stood at the centre of time and space, at the centre of the world, and the Emperor's presence within it signified the immanent presence of God at the heart of all things, the Logos manifest at the primordial point of which all things are a development or an expansion. In this sense, the Emperor in his Palace is attached by analogy to the original mystery, that mystery of the genesis of the world from the Divine Unity, invisible and non-manifest. It is by virtue of God's unmoved and unified presence at the centre that the multiplicity of 'the wheel of becoming' exists; so, too, it is by virtue of the Emperor's unmoved solitary presence in his palace that the many-sided aspects of the human and social order within his orbit revolve in harmony. And as God manifests himself not directly to humanity, but through the hierarchies of Cherubim and Seraphim, the cohorts of angels, the ranks of the super-terrestrial principalities and powers, so the Emperor is surrounded also by the whole hierarchy of court dignitaries, the numberless ranks of officials civil and military—the patricians and the *magistroi*, the *spatharioi* and the *protospatharioi*, the *logothetes* and the *strategoi*, the silentiaries and the chartularies, the host of *cubicularii*, eunuchs in imitation of the indifferent sexuality of the angelic host—who do his bidding on land and sea, manifest his central presence to the extreme bounds of his terrestrial kingdom, arrange his appearances, receive his guests, govern his themes, keep his purse, guard his robes, distribute his justice, examine the petitions made to him, maintain his stables and his estates, minister to his flocks and herds, command his fleets, and attend to all the other endless details of imperial administration, from leading an army against the enemy through the desperate plains of Cilicia, the scorched solitudes of the Euphrates and the Orontes, or the winter fastness of the Bulgarian hinterland, to helping the Emperor mount his horse or to placing the imperial spear on the necks of prostrate captives.

Monogram of Christ in the form of a wheel from the paten of Bishop Paternus, about 520. Hermitage, Leningrad.

It was within the walls of this sacred precinct that, regulated by the many palace time-pieces, sun-dials or water-clocks, the daily ritual unfolded. At dawn the main doors to the Palace were unlocked. With three knocks on the door of his private apartments the Emperor was roused. Dressed, he entered the throne-room, prayed before the icon. Those with whom he had business to conduct, or to whom he was to give an audience, were then presented to him. If the audience were given to some important personage, or group of personages, to, say, the envoys of a foreign prince, it might be conducted with all the extravagant paraphernalia of an epiphany, a divine appearance. So it was, for instance, on the occasion of the reception, held in the great hall of the Magnaura under Constantine and Romanus Porphyrogenitoi, of the Saracen ambassadors from Tarsus. Silvered chains of copper, borrowed from a monastic church, were hung on either side of the hall, and from them were suspended great golden candelabra taken from a palatine church. On the right side of the hall, between the pillars, stood a golden organ, with two other organs of the two factions, the Greens and the Blues, on either side. A line of trees planted for a walk or shade down the centre of the Magnaura was made into a covered passage by means of silk awnings. On either side of the pillars, palace hangings fell in soft folds from these awnings to the ground. All the floors were strewn with ivy and laurel, or, in the more private apartments, with myrtle and rosemary, while that of the Magnaura itself was petalled with roses, so that, trodden underfoot by the courtiers, their crushed essence might fill the air with sweetness. Costly Persian carpets lay at the entrances. Right and left of the imperial throne, the 'throne of Solomon', stood the court officials known as *candidatoi*, Roman sceptres in their hands. Above the steps leading to the throne, a company of men was stationed with the Emperor's silken, gold-embroidered banner, while others near these men held other golden imperial banners. Above stood the choristers from the churches of the Holy Apostles and St. Sophia, who acclaimed and sang the imperial odes as the Emperor entered the hall. This he did robed in his octagonal *chlamys*, decorated perhaps with great golden circles enclosing flowers or fleurons in gold, rosettes or heart-shaped ornaments, and wearing a white diadem. As he took his seat on the throne of Solomon, all around him wished him long life and prosperous times. Then the Saracen envoys entered, supported by the Captain of the Palace and the Master of the Horse, wearing the robes, with embroidery and tassels, that the Emperor had ordered for the occasion. What happened at this juncture we may learn from an account of another audience, left by Luidprand, future bishop of Cremona, who as envoy of Berenger II, king of Italy (950–961), was received, in the company of some Spanish envoys, by Constantine Porphyrogenitus in the same hall of the Magnaura:

Before the Emperor's seat stood a tree, made of bronze gilded over, whose branches were filled with birds, also made of gilded bronze, which uttered different cries, each according to its varying species. The throne itself was so marvellously fashioned that at one moment it seemed a low structure, and at another it rose high into the air. It was of immense size and was guarded by lions, made either of bronze or of wood covered over with gold, who beat the ground with their tails and gave a dreadful roar with open mouth and quivering tongue. Leaning upon the shoulders of two eunuchs I was brought into the Emperor's presence. At my approach the lions began to roar and the birds to cry out, each according to its kind; but I was neither terrified nor surprised, for I had previously made enquiry about all these things from people who were well acquainted with them. So after I had three times made obeisance to the Emperor with my face upon the ground, I lifted my head, and behold! the man who just before I had seen sitting on a moderately elevated seat had now changed his raiment and was sitting on the level of the ceiling. How it was done I could not imagine, unless perhaps he was lifted up by some sort of device as we use for raising the timbers of a wine press. On that occasion he did not address me personally, since even if he had wanted to do so the wide distance between us would have rendered conversation unseemly, but by the intermediary of a secretary he enquired about Berenger's doings and asked after his health. I made a fitting reply and then, at a nod from the interpreter, left his presence and retired to my lodging. [28]

The receptions would continue, with the same ceremonial, also in the afternoon, after an interval in the middle of the day when the palatine doors were again closed. In the evening there might be a banquet. Should it be one of the twelve days between Christmas and Epiphany, when the Emperor gave a series of feasts, this would be held in the large reception hall, the Tribunal of the Nineteen Couches. Seated at a gold table, the Emperor, in imitation of Christ and the Apostles, was surrounded by twelve chosen guests, while the rest of the company was disposed in groups of twelve at the remaining eighteen tables. Again it is Liudprand who has left a description of one such banquet, typical of many that must have taken place:

There is a palace near the Hippodrome looking northwards, wonderfully lofty and beautiful, which is called 'Decannea Cubita', 'the hall of the nineteen couches'. The reason of its name is obvious: 'deca' is Greek for ten,

Byzantine woven silk material from the so-called eagle-chasuble of St. Albuin in the cathedral treasury of Bressanone (Brixen), dating from the tenth or eleventh century.

'ennea' for nine, and 'cubita' are couches with curved ends; and on the day when Our Lord Jesus Christ was born according to the flesh nineteen covers were always laid here at the table. The Emperor and his guests on this occasion do not sit at dinner, as they usually do, but recline on couches; and everything is served in vessels, not of silver, but of gold. After the solid food fruit is brought on in three golden bowls, which are too heavy for men to lift and come in on carriers covered over with a purple cloth. Two of them are put on the table in the following way. Through openings in the ceiling hang ropes covered with gilded leather and furnished with golden rings. These rings are attached to the handles projecting from the bowls, and with four or five men helping from below, they are swung on to the table by means of a moveable device in the ceiling and removed again in the same fashion. [29]

After the meal, which Luidprand seems to have enjoyed, except perhaps for the wine ('the Greek wine we found undrinkable', he remarks elsewhere, 'because of the mixture in it of pitch, resin, and plaster'), there were the entertainments:

As for the various entertainments I saw there, it would be too long to describe them all, and so for the moment I pass them by. One, however, was so remarkable that it will not be out of place to insert an account of it here.

A man came in carrying on his head, without using his hands, a wooden pole twenty-four feet or more long, which a foot and a half from the top had a cross piece three feet wide. Then two boys appeared, naked except for loin cloths round their middle, who went up the pole, did various tricks on it, and then came down head first, keeping the pole all the time steady as though it were rooted in the earth. When one had come down, the other remained on the pole and performed by himself, which filled me with even greater astonishment and admiration. While they were both performing their feat seemed hardly possible; for, wonderful as it was, the evenness of their weights kept the pole up which they climbed balanced. But when one remained at the top and kept his balance so accurately that he could both do his tricks and come down again without mishap, I was so bewildered that the Emperor himself noticed my astonishment. He therefore called an interpreter, and asked me which seemed the more wonderful, the boy who had moved so carefully that the pole remained firm, or the man who had so deftly balanced it on his head that neither the boys' weight nor their performance had disturbed it in the least. I said that I did not know which I thought plus merveilleux, *more wonderful; and he burst into a loud laugh and said he was in the same case, he did not know either.* [30]

Thus might the Emperor's day end. Or it might be then that he would continue late into the night, at prayer, or writing, or studying official documents, conferring with his advisers, meditating on the vast and complex affairs of state. So worked for instance the great Justinian; and it was at such hours as these that, according to Procopius, sometimes those who were with him would see him rise suddenly from the throne and pace up and down the long echoing hall; and as he paced his head would mysteriously disappear, and his body would continue pacing during the time—it might have been a matter of several hours—that passed before his head would return again to his shoulders; or they would see his eyes vanish from their sockets and his face become featureless flesh.

*

The Emperor, however, was not the sole figure round whom these palatine ceremonies and functions revolved. There was also the Empress: 'When there is no Augusta', writes a Byzantine historian, 'it is impossible to celebrate the festivals and to give the feasts prescribed by the etiquette.' The Empress was by no means simply a passive figure in the imperial drama, a recluse severely cloistered in the *gynaeceum*, or women's quarter, guarded by eunuchs and only attended by her ladies-in-waiting, beardless men, or venerable priests; displayed but on rare ceremonial occasions and then beneath thick veils. On the contrary, she was the Emperor's feminine counterpart, the true queen, *basilissa*, the elect of God, royal image of the feminine aspects of the Divinity, of the divine Beauty and Consolation that held in balance the masculine image of the divine Majesty and Justice fulfilled by the *basileus*. Even in the normal fashion of her choice elements of the supernatural came into play: here it was no dynastic consideration, the need to cement an alliance with a foreign power, or other such expedient, that determined her selection; instead, throughout the imperial territories, through the lands and cities of the Caucasus and Greece, Syria and Paphlagonia, Cappadocia and the Balkans, a search was made for those who in beauty, grace of manner, and intelligence seemed most fit for the high calling. Likely candidates were brought to Constantinople and there, as the three Graces before Paris, were exposed to the Emperor's scrutiny, when one would be singled out for the apple of preference. Even where the selection was less deliberate;

where the Emperor, as Justinian by the bearkeeper's prostitute daughter Theodora, with her delicate oval face and her solemn staring eyes, was led captive more drastically, this same providential element seems to enter in and determine the choice.

Once chosen, by whatever means, the ritual of coronation and marriage consolidated the Empress in her more-than-mortal station. As if indicating that her exaltation to her office was the consequence of divine intervention and not due to or dependent on the Emperor, the coronation was celebrated before the marriage, though both took place on the same day: she was, that is, invested with sovereignty before becoming the wife of the *basileus*. The ceremonies took place in the Palace. The insignia of office were laid on a portable altar where the Patriarch and his clergy took their stand. At a command from the Emperor, the Empress, lighted candles in her hand, was brought in. The Patriarch read a prayer over the sacred imperial *chlamys*, handed it to the Emperor, who, while the *cubicularii* shielded the Empress with the over-garment previously removed, now put it on her. The Patriarch recited a prayer over the Empress' crown and ornaments, the strings of pearl and precious stones that hung from the crown down to the neck, and again the Emperor put them on the Empress. Now the new sovereign presented herself to her people. This too she did alone, without the Emperor. Escorted only by her chamberlains and ladies-in-waiting she made her way slowly between the ranks of soldiers of the guard, senators, patricians, high dignitaries, through the apartments of the Palace, until she reached the terrace below which were gathered the living body of the State, the army and the people. With her rich, gold-embroidered imperial costume hiding the contours of her body, she showed herself to her subjects and by her subjects was solemnly recognized, as they cried: 'Holy! Holy! Holy! Glory to God in the highest! Peace on earth!' Alone, aloof she stood, candle in hand, and bowed first to the Cross, and then, while all prostrated themselves and standards were dipped, to the right and left in salutation of her people. Then, pursued by the acclamations of the crowd, 'Lord, strengthen the Empire!', 'God, save the Augusta!', she made her way back through the Palace to the church of St. Stephen, where her marriage was to be celebrated.

The Patriarch again presided over the ritual, in which Emperor and Empress were crowned with nuptial crowns. With these on their heads, and attended by the high functionaries of the court, they made their way to the nuptial chamber, while organs and cymbals sounded, and the chanters sang the praises and acclamations: 'Many and long years! Welcome, sovereign of the Romans! Welcome, Augusta, elect of God! Welcome, Augusta, protected by God! Welcome, you who rejoice the hearts of the Romans! Welcome, you who share the purple! Welcome, you whom all desire!' To these laudatory epithalamiums Emperor and Empress laid their crowns on the royal bed. Then groom and bride partook of the wedding feast. Three days later, the new *basilissa* took her sacred bath. Accompanied by her court, acclaimed by the factions, to the sound of music, the Empress amid her cortège made her way to the bathing-place. On each side of the Empress walked three ladies-in-waiting carrying three pomegranates, symbols of fertility, studded with precious stones. Other women carried fine linen, boxes of perfume, bowls. While the Empress was taking her bath, all waited outside to conduct her back to the bridal chamber.

The Empress now found herself in a position from which she might exercise considerable influence, private and political. She was the virtual mistress of her own court in the vast apartments of the imperial *gynaeceum*, with a host of servitors and dignitaries, the Grand Chamberlain at their head, at her command. Her numerous ladies-in-waiting, presided over by the Grand Mistress of the Palace, chosen though they may have been by the Emperor, were generally invested also by the Empress at a personal ceremony at which they received their official court dress—golden tunic, white mantle, a high, tower-like coiffure from which hung a long white veil. She had in addition her private fortune, to administer as she would, without consulting the Emperor. She assisted the Emperor when foreign princesses visited

The Emperor Justinian beside Bishop Maximian. Section of a mosaic from the first half of the sixth century in the choir of San Vitale at Ravenna.

the court; like the Emperor, she gave audiences, held banquets, and gave gifts. She attended court dinners with the Emperor, was present at the Hippodrome courses. It was she also who, in the women's gallery of St. Sophia, after the Resurrection service gave the kiss of peace to all the wives and widows of imperial dignitaries in the same hierarchical order as the Emperor below, in the main body of the church, was receiving the male members of the imperial service.

How in fact from her position she chose to exercise the influence at her disposal, or whether she chose to exercise it at all, was very much a matter of her own temperament. All types of women were to be found among these Byzantine Augustae. Some, like Justinian's Theodora, combining her pale beauty with a superiority of intelligence, were masterful creatures, with all the terrible pride of those driven by extreme inner tension beyond the limits of human patience. It was Theodora who, again according to Procopius, used to keep high officials waiting for audience in a stuffy room: 'When after many days of waiting some of them were summoned to an audience, they were quickly dismissed after prostrating themselves and kissing her feet. They were not permitted to say a word or make any petition unless she bade them.'[31] Tales were told of secret private dungeons in her palace where people disappeared for

The Empress Theodora with attendants.
Section of a mosaic on the opposite wall
of the same choir.

ever; and certainly she was able to shelter Anthimus, deposed from the patriarchal throne for mono-physite leanings, for twelve years in her apartments without anyone knowing he was there: he was only discovered, in perfect health, after her death. But it was also Theodora who took part in framing imperial laws; who sought to prevent the traffic in young girls in the city; who built hospitals and orphanages; who at the time of the Nika Rebellion made the speech that held Justinian from flight: *I hold that now if ever flight is inexpedient even if it brings safety. When a man has once been born into the light it is inevitable that he should also meet death. But for an Emperor to become a fugitive is not a thing to be endured.... If you wish to flee to safety, Emperor, it can easily be done. We have money in plenty; there is the sea; here are the ships. But as for me, I hold with the old saying that royalty makes a fine winding-sheet.*[32] Passionate and despotic, complex and disconcerting, endlessly seductive, Theodora, for the twenty years that she reigned (she died, in middle age, of cancer), exercised her authority everywhere, filling the administration with her protégés, making and unmaking Popes and Patriarchs, ministers and generals, ardent in the cause of those she favoured, merciless towards those who thwarted, or sought to thwart, her plans, and using, to execute her vengeance, all means: force and perfidy, lies and corruption, intrigue and violence. Her memory, with that of her husband Justinian, is celebrated by the Church on 14 November; and her portrait, facing that of Justinian, is in the apse of the church of San Vitale at Ravenna, where, elegantly toileted and followed by female attendants, she wears a cloak of purple violet with a broad hem of gold, and there is a halo round her head, and from her hair cascades of pearls and precious stones fall to her shoulders.

Few other Empresses had the consuming intensity of Theodora, but many had qualities that made them remarkable. There was the ageing Zoë (1028–1050), for instance, who although past seventy had not a wrinkle on her face, but was as fresh as she had been in the prime of her beauty. Golden-haired, white-skinned, her hands *had never busied themselves with a distaff, nor did she ever work at a loom or any other feminine occupation. Still more surprising, she affected scorn for the beautiful dressses of her rank.... Her one concern at this time, the thing on which she spent all her energy, was the development of new species of perfumes, or the preparation of unguents. Some she would invent, others she improved. Her own private bedroom was no more impressive than the workshop in the market where the artisans and blacksmiths toil, for all round the room were burning braziers, a host of them....* [33] Withal, she was of extreme piety: 'her passionate veneration for the things of God had really brought her into contact, so to speak, with the First and Purest Light. Certainly there was no moment when the Name of God was not on her lips'. [34] Another Empress of extreme piety was Irene Doukas, wife of the Emperor Alexis I Comnenus (1081–1118); her daughter, Anna, herself one of the most intellectual of all Byzantine princesses, has written of this: *I remember the Empress, my mother, when breakfast was ready on the table carrying a book in her hands and poring over the writings of the didactic Fathers, especially those of the philosopher and martyr Maximus. For she was not so much interested in the physical disputations as in those about the dogmas, because she wished to gain true wisdom. And I was often seized with wonder at her and one day in my wonder I said to her: 'How can you spontaneously rise to such sublime heights? for I tremble and dare not listen to such things even with the tips of my ears. For the purely abstract and intellectual character of the man makes one's head swim, as the saying goes.' She smiled and said: 'I know that kind of quite laudable dread; and I myself do not touch these books without a tremor and yet I cannot tear myself away from them. But you wait a little and after you have dipped into other books, you will taste the sweetness of these.'* [35] Yet another Empress, Theophano, unwilling wife of Leo VI (886–912), retired to a monastery, and through the holiness of her life is now one of the saints of the Church. Not so her namesake, wife first of Romanus II Porphyrogenitus (959–963), then, on his death, of Nicephorus Phocas (Emperor 963–969): beautiful, extravagantly seductive, restlessly ambitious. It was in her apartments of the Palace that was hatched the plot which led to the assassination of Nicephorus by her lover, John Tzimisces, though her gain from this was not a third imperial husband, as she had intended, but monastic exile; for Tzimisces, faced by the Patriarch with the choice between the throne and Theophano, chose the first, and banished the second from the city.

So on this imperial stage the Empress plays out her allotted part beside the Emperor, fulfilling, whatever her private and personal deviations, the public and impersonal image of his feminine counterpart, involved in the same ritual, consecrated to the same destiny, transcending the frailty of her nature in the exalted dignity of her calling, once even occupying the imperial throne herself, and signing state documents, with the masculine title of the office, 'great *basileus* and autocrat of the Romans'. We catch a final glimpse of her when, in 1432, shortly before the Empire, straitened and impoverished, was overthrown, Bertrandon de la Brocquière visited Constantinople and saw her as she came from St. Sophia after the divine service:

The Empress, daughter to the Emperor of Trebizond, seemed very handsome, but as I was at a distance I wished to have a nearer view; and I was also desirous to see how she mounted her horse, for it was thus she had come to the church, attended only by two ladies, three old men, ministers of state, and three of that species of men to whose guard the Turks entrust their wives.... At length she appeared. A bench was brought forth and placed near her horse, which was superb, and had a magnificent saddle. When she had mounted the bench, one of the old men took the long mantle she wore, passed to the opposite side of the horse, and held it in his hands extended as high as he could; during this, she put her foot in the stirrup, and bestrode the horse like a man. When she was in her seat, the old man cast the mantle over her shoulders; after which, one of those long hats with a point, so common in Greece, was given to her; it was ornamented at one of the extremities with three golden plumes, and was very becoming. I was so near that I was ordered to fall back, and, consequently, had a full view of her. She wore in her ears broad and flat rings, set with several precious stones, especially rubies. She looked young and fair, and handsomer than when in church. In one word, I should not have had a fault to find with her, had she not been painted, and assuredly she had not any need of it. The two ladies mounted their horses at the same time that she did; they were both handsome, and wore, like her, mantles and hats. The company returned to the Palace....[36]

*

The Emperor's ceremonial life, with or without the Empress, was by no means confined to the Palace. If within the Palace it is the static aspects of imperial iconography that dominate, those of the Emperor as the invariable centre round which all human affairs, the whole 'wheel of becoming', revolve, outside other aspects of his role come into their own: here the Emperor appears as the triumphant conqueror, defender and champion of the faith, active propagator of the Word of God over the territories of the world, redeeming, by force of arms if needs be, lands and peoples still living in 'outer darkness' beyond the imperial frontiers for the chosen nation, the new Israel of the Christian Empire. It was here that the incredible brilliance of imperial pageantry was exploited to the full. Sometimes the Emperor himself would take the field, moving off from the palatine port of Boucoleon in his galley to join the army assembled on the other side of the Bosphorus, his expeditionary baggage of dining tent and sleeping tent (two of each); of stoves, water-heaters, chandeliers, and candles; medicaments, massage-unguents, perfumes, and sweet-smelling pastilles; table linen, uniforms, underwear, arms, and insignia; silver clock and writing parchment; chapel and icons and portable altar and sacred vessels; travelling library on war, weather, portents, and religion; oils, wines, vegetables, cheese, salt, fish, and caviare, with their animate complement of sheep, cows, goats, geese, and chickens: all the equipment of imperial travel down to the water-beakers for the chickens when on horseback, packed where possible into immense copper chests with iron fittings and loaded on to a train of 685 horses and mules, each branded with the royal mark and caparisoned in scarlet. At other times he would not himself lead his army but, his place delegated to a general, would preside over its departure from the capital city. Thus would Romanus II have presided when Nicephorus Phocas set out with the imperial army and fleet to recapture Crete from the Saracens. On that summer's day of 960 the whole waters between the Golden Horn and the slopes of Chrysopolis and Chalcedon, with their palaces and villas, would have been packed with thousands of ships, according to some as many as 3,300, their sides painted vivid colours, their bright sails tinted a hundred distinct shades, their great standards bearing the images of the Mother of God, of Christos Pantocrator, of the military saints St. George, St. Demetrius, St. Theodorus Stratilates. On the bridges of ships the brilliant costumes of all the races of the East mingled with the more sombre clothing—animal hides and fur—worn by the sons of the North and the warriors of the Steppes. The voices of Turmach and Drungarios, of Topoteretis and Centarch mixed and clashed as the heavy transports were manoeuvred, the last troops embarked. Hundreds of small boats, caïques painted blue or vermilion, crossed and recrossed from one ship to another, their passengers clothed in the bright apparel of the Byzantine nobility, silk embroidered with gold and silver. On the two shores, palaces and villas, churches and towers, terraces shaded by tall trees, the long lines of crenelated walls, were crowded with onlookers. Behind the high grills of the Palace gardens, in the depths of the immense *gynaeceum*, the *basilissa*, in the full pride of her station, surrounded by all her ladies-in-waiting, her slaves, her patricians *zostae*, the *spatharissae*, the *stratorissae*, the *hypatissae*, guarded by eunuchs, watched from her throne. Below them, at the magnificent port of the imperial residence, the Boucoleon, made entirely by man's hand, its marble quays and lavish steps covered with columns and statues, the young Emperor and his court, with the Patriarch and the high clergy and all the members of the Holy Synod, with the Senate and the chief dignitaries clothed in gold or silk, coiffed with caps of gold brocade, had taken their place on the improvised platform. Martial music rose, savage and strange: the raw, terrifying blast of trumpet, the cadenced beat of cymbals, the brief precipitate roll of drums, the war-songs of all the barbarian races, the interminable acclamations of the factions, official, bizarre, regulated; while in all the churches and oratories monks and choristers intoned the hymn to the All-Holy Hodigitria, to the Invincible Champion, the breachless wall, the City's safeguard, Mary. Then suddenly silence falls; the Patriarch gives the blessing; the *basileus*, standing, makes a sign; and, as the acclamations resound along the shores of two continents, the immense fleet unfolds slowly out into the Sea of Marmara.[37]

Still more impressive must have been the return of the victorious *basileus* from war, when, bearing the insignia of royalty, chief among them the *labarum*, wearing on his shoulders a blue gold-bordered *chlamys*, while a violet tunic, also bordered with gold, sown with leaves of ivy and trefoil, hung down to his knees, golden belted, scarlet buskins on his feet, the harness and saddle of his white horse glittering with pearls and precious stones, his brilliant escort about him, the Emperor rode from the Golden Gate through the flower-strewn streets of the city, between the houses hung with enormous Babylonian tapestries and incomparable Persian embroideries, to the central square of the Augustaeum, acclaimed by the people, welcomed by Patriarch and Prefect. Or again of equal magnificence was the official celebration of an imperial triumph: here the Emperor seated himself at the top of the tiers surrounding the huge column in the forum of Constantine, the Patriarch beside him, while the prisoners of war and their conquered standards and *flamoula*, each held by a herald, were lined up in the Praetorion facing them, or in the Senate. Then at a signal a high official, the Protonotarios of the Course, made them advance into the middle of the Forum, where they were ranged in the sun's glare. Then, in the silence, the first imperial chanter began to intone with tense quivering voice the verses of the great Byzantine hymn of victory, that which Moses and the children of Israel sang after deliverance from the land of Egypt: 'I will sing unto the Lord, for he hath triumphed gloriously: the horse and his rider has he thrown into the sea. The Lord is my strength and song, and he is become my salvation.... The Lord is a man of war....' And the whole company of chanters and the entire people replied in chorus to the soloist. The hymn over, the Logothete of the Course, another senior official, in some senses a kind of Minister of Foreign Affairs, the Domestic of the Schools, high-ranking commander of the palatine guards, the *strategoi* or governors of provinces who happened to be staying in the capital, the Drungarios of the imperial fleet, or again the archons or first officers of the fleet, the Turmachs and other leading provincial functionaries, seized the principal prisoners, barbarian kings or Saracen emirs, and dragged them to the foot of the Emperor's stand; and there the chief prisoner was thrown to the ground and his head was placed beneath the feet of the *basileus*, motionless in his superior indifference as he set his right foot, shod in the scarlet buskin, on the shaved skull of the humiliated captive; while the Protostrator, the chief equerry, laid on the back of his neck the iron of the lance which the *basileus* carried in his right hand. And at this solemn moment, when the dethroned sovereign or defeated general drank to the bitter dregs the cup of his humiliation, and when the Autocrator radiated all the might of his universal majesty, the other prisoners, at an order from their guards, fell to the ground, conquered lances and standards were dipped, again the voice of the solo chanter sounded: 'Who is great like our God? You are the God who performs miracles', and the great prayer, of triumph and thanksgiving, rose to the sky, with the people crying between each verse *Kyrie eleison*....

*

If these ceremonies relate to the *basileus* in his capacity as representative of the Lord of Hosts, as active defender of the faith, wielder of the sword of righteousness over the heads of the infidels, and as such are largely military in character, while those within the Palace image the Divinity more as the 'unmoved first mover', there is yet a third category which shows forth the Emperor in relationship with the cosmos and its people, as the cosmic king. These are the ceremonies in the Hippodrome, those popular celebrations in which ruler and people participate in the spectacle of the endless circling 'play of life', the great game of existence in the world. As so many other aspects of Byzantine life, so this aspect was originally pregnant with its own symbolism, inherited from Rome. The Hippodrome itself was an image of the cosmos. The arena was the earth, the channel of water—the *euripus*—running between the arena and the first tier of seats was the ocean; the twelve doors of the boxes from which the chariots issued were the twelve signs of the zodiac. Along the *spina* were the solar obelisks and the Delphic monument of Helios Apollo. As Helios, the Sun, so each chariot was drawn by four horses, and each course, which imitated the supposed course of the sun, was seven times round, completing thus the sun's weekly revolutions. The four factions competing represented the four elements: green, earth; blue, water; red, fire; white, air, with their corresponding seasons in the annual cycle: spring, summer, autumn, winter. And the imperial gesture signalling the opening of the games was in imitation of the original divine gesture setting in motion the whole cosmic process. In this way the Hippodrome repeated in another form many of the symbolic elements inherent in the theocratic idea: that as the whole universe revolved round and was regulated by the immovable Deity, so all human society, the whole multitudinous circle of life, revolved round and was regulated by the Emperor.

We have already noted what a central part the Hippodrome in fact played in the life of the people of the imperial capital. As has been said[38], it was here that Emperors were made and unmade, that justice was meted out and the guilty punished, that triumphs over barbarian and rebel were celebrated, that nature and art were admired, that religion and superstition, the love of glory and the sense of the beautiful, were indulged in. The virtues and the vices of these people, pagan in their Christianity, vain in their humiliation, were here satisfied. The Hippodrome was not only a circus; it was also a theatre, a theatre in which was played in living terms many of the phases and facets, plots and counterplots, of the vivid existence of the city's populace. And it was above all here that this populace came face to face with the *basileus*, that the king sat in festive state among his subject people.

When the day marked for the celebration of the games in the Hippodrome approached, the whole city was astir. The factions completed their arrangements, saw that all was prepared. On the eve of the great day, an imperial herald came to the Hippodrome and ordered the *velum* to be suspended above the imperial box: it was in this way that the solemnity was announced. Then the day itself came. Everything in the city was closed, and through the gates into the Hippodrome the crowds poured, native and foreigner, citizen and peasant, nobleman and artisan: the hardy highlander from the Rhodope mountains and the pirate of the Archipelago; Bosphorus boatman and shipyard worker from the Golden Horn; merchant from Hungary and Armenian conscript. In special reserved seats sat the ambassadors of foreign nations, *missi dominici* from a Western king side by side with the ambassadors from the Persian court. In the rows of seats closest to the arena, whose fresh yellow sand was mingled with the odorous dust of the cedar and strewn with flowers, sat the members of the factions, their white tunics bordered with large strips of purple, their scarves showing their rival colours, holding a baton surmounted by a cross. The great silk *velum* floated in the breeze above the imperial box. The sound of organ music rose. The boxes to the right and left of the imperial box filled with generals, senators, patricians. Behind the windows of the women's gallery of the palatine church of St. Stephen might be sensed the presence of the Empress and her court. Finally, the Emperor appeared in his tribune, sceptre in hand, crown on head, and with the hem of his imperial cloak gathered in his hand he made the sign of the cross over his people, three times, once to the centre, once to the right over the Blues, once to the left over the Greens. It was time for the opening signal, the fiat, to set the microcosmic scene in motion.

It was given. Beneath the imperial tribune four doors opened, four barriers were lowered, four chariots drawn by four swift coursers leapt into the arena, their four colours, green and blue, red and white, clearly visible. Upright in the cockpits of their chariots stood the charioteers, leaning forward over their horses, arms working furiously, the sand flying beneath them. And now the cries of the factions rose, shouts of encouragement, prayers for victory: 'O God, protect the Emperor, protect the Magistrates, protect the children born in the purple, protect the Prefect of the city .... O God, protect Olympios, protect Porphyrius, give them victory, give victory to the Blues. Mother of God, may they win, that the Empire be filled with joy, that we dance the dance of triumph....' To such cries, to the frantic cheers of the members of the winning faction, to the howls of dismay from their rivals, the race ends, the victor is declared. Then once more the sand is levelled, once more the doors open, and the next race begins. After the fourth race came the interval. There were entertainments: clowns, acrobats, parades of strange animals. In front of the imperial box a spokesman of one of the factions might be voicing some popular grievance to the Emperor, carrying on an improvised dialogue, a kind of chant obeying definite metrical rules, with the imperial herald who answered for the Emperor.

Meanwhile, as this dialogue was going on in the arena, other spectators might promenade round the high porticos above the tiers of seats, looking out over the magnificent scene of the city and its setting; over the silver roofs and golden domes of palaces and churches; over the great streets bordered with porticos; over the triumphal arches and the bronze columns topped by their statues of Emperor and Empress; over the cypresses and sycamores of palatine and monastic gardens; over the waters of the Bosphorus filled with the billowing sails of the ships of all nations; over the summer palaces on the Asiatic coast, the blue of the Sea of Marmara rippled here and there in the light harvesting wind or broken by the black lunge and dip of a dolphin; across finally to the far mountains of Bithynia shimmering in the haze: over all this immense capital, restless compound of Greece and Rome, of Christ and Caesar, of Europe and Asia, metropolis of commerce and centre of culture, queen of the world's cities whose seductive image could both summon from nothing when time was ripe those other imperial cities, Ravenna, Venice, Kiev, Moscow, even Vienna, and conjure its own downfall in the minds of Latin Christian and Turkish Moslem alike. Well might the Byzantine in his Hippodrome feel himself truly to be at the centre of the universe, at the hub of life's turning wheel.

Down on the rows of marble seats below, hampers and packages of food would be unpacked—dried meat, salted fish, cooked beans, water-melons, lemons and oranges. If the games were being held on 11 May, the anniversary of the city's dedication, on the eve of the festival heaps of vegetables and cakes would have been piled in the Hippodrome. After the races, when the victorious charioteers had received their laurel crowns, and the Emperor had risen to take lunch, the crowds descended and set upon the provisions he had granted them. A large *caïque* was then drawn round the arena on a cart and from it dried fish were thrown. The fare was frugal, even if it was at the Emperor's expense. *This meagre feast*, writes Rambaud, *hardly recalls the fabulous* congiaria *which Caesar, after his triumphs, offered the Roman*

people seated round forty thousand tables, where nothing seemed delectable enough for the palate of the sovereign people, where the wines of Greece and Sicily were poured out by the cupful to the labourers and lazzaroni of Rome. The rare viands thrown into the Tiber on the morrow of one of these orgies to which the Caesars invited the entire nation would have glutted these sober Byzantine drinkers of water-melon.

The time had now come to resume the races. The factions grew impatient. Chants were directed at the imperial box, inviting the Emperor to return from lunch, to give the signal for the afternoon session to open: 'Rise, Imperial Sun, arise, appear!' If he failed to come, the chants became less and less respectful. On one occasion at least their abusiveness was such that the Emperor sent his guards in with sabre, whip, and baton among the people. Normally, though, he would return promptly, eager as his people to share the excitements of the afternoon, to see once more the furious chariots plunge through the swirling sand, to hear the thunderous hooves, to watch his favourite driver outstrip his rivals and strike for the winning-post: Constantius, who deserved a golden gift for his merit, or the great Porphyrius, on whom nature had bestowed all the grace she had....

On the two following pages: *Vedute* (panorama) of Constantinople from the work of Anselme Bandurri: Imperium Orientale, Paris 1711.

69

Chateau des Sept Tours

Tour de Bellissaire

Fanari kiosk

Port de Calcedoine

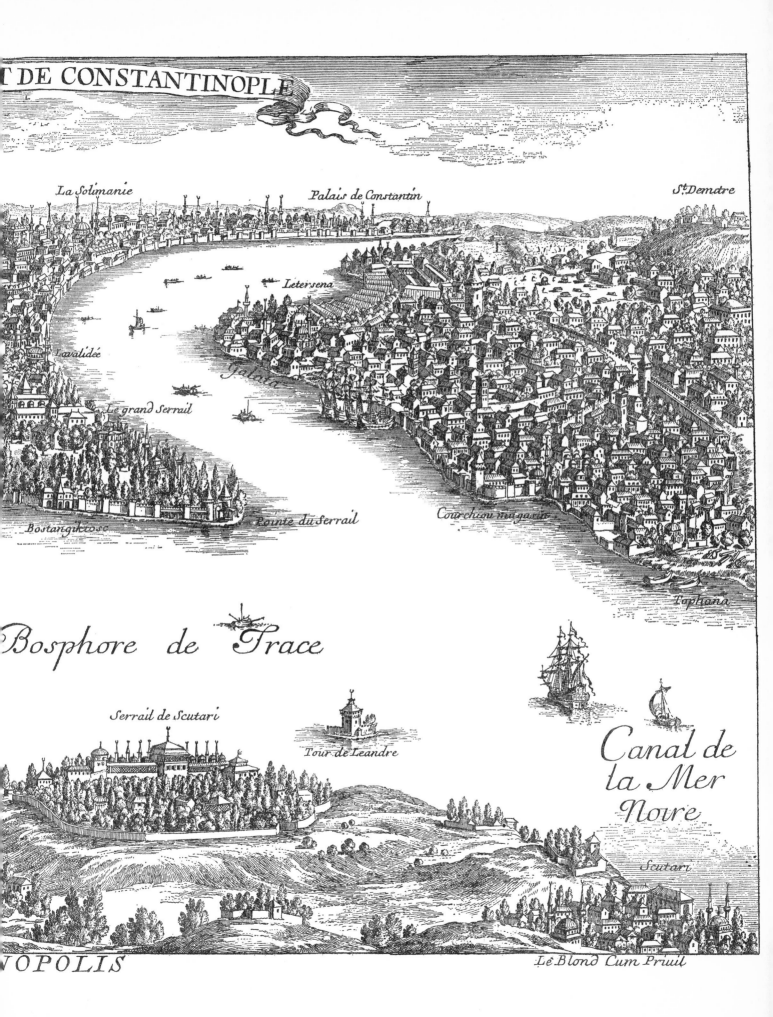

T DE CONSTANTINOPLE

La Solimanie   Palais de Constantin   St Demetre

Letersena

Lavalidée

Galata

Le grand Serrail

Bostangikiosc   Pointe du Serrail   Courchiou magazin

Taphana

Bosphore de Trace

Serrail de Scutari

Tour de Leandre

Canal de la Mer Noire

Scutari

NOPOLIS   Le Blond Cum Priuil

All these ceremonies; this whole elaborate imperial etiquette centring on the Sacred Palace and the person of the Emperor, with its order and its offices, its vestments and its chants, its sanctuaries and iconography: these impressive parades and solemn triumphs, palatine receptions and public games, these banquets, pomps, and spectacles: all were directed to establishing and conserving the exalted conception of the imperial office. Moreover, they were, both in their symbolic connotations and in their ritual details, from the solar imagery down to the use of candles and incense, largely a repetition of Roman imperial models, overlaid as these might be with a veneer of Christian terminology and practice. This meant that if in them the Emperor was officially the vice-regent of Christ, he was none the less fulfilling this role by acting the part of Caesar—a part which Christ himself had explicitly refused to act when he allowed himself to be handed over to the Jews: 'My kingdom is not of this world: if my kingdom were of this world, then would my servants fight, that I should not be delivered to the Jews.' [39] Leaving on one side for the moment the question of whether or to what extent the role of Caesar could legitimately be assimilated to that of Christ, there was a whole other series of ceremonies in which the Emperor, without in the least renouncing his exalted status, showed himself in a relationship that revealed how different his position was, at least in theory, from that of Caesar; revealed how, far from being himself a divinity, his very election to and occupation of the imperial office depended on his servitude to the Incarnate God; how the origin and condition of his status was a continual act of submission. This series of ceremonies consisted of those strictly Christian ceremonies that were an integral part of the liturgical life of the Church, and they followed the annual cycle of festivals which composed the Christian calendar: the Annunciation, the services of Holy Week, the Ascension and Pentecost, the Transfiguration, the Dormition of the Virgin, the Exaltation of the Precious and Life-Giving Cross, the Nativity, the Epiphany, all the commemorative feasts of the Apostles, saints, and martyrs. But it was perhaps in the Divine Liturgy itself that the corporate life of the Church found its fullest expression. Here, in this public cult, social and visible, Emperor and people renewed each Sunday their, and the Empire's, dedication to the invisible Kingdom of the God who is both One and Trinitarian, the Father, Son, and Holy Spirit; of his saints and angels; and especially of his Holy Mother, the Theotokos. Here Emperor and people were reminded that their titles, honours, and even citizenship depended not merely on their membership of a terrestrial city but on their subscription to the Christian faith; that their true patrimony was their religion. Here Church and State, the clergy, the people, and their sovereign, made manifest their existence as a single social and political body, a holy nation, chosen under God and dedicated to his service. 'We thy servants, O Christ, bring to thee of thine own, praying that thou wilt graciously accept it, O Son and Logos of God, made flesh and crucified for us. Strengthen us in the true faith, increase and guard this state which thou hast entrusted to us, through the mediation of Mary, the holy Virgin, the Mother of God.' Thus ran, we are told, the words which Justinian and Theodora inscribed round the golden altar of St. Sophia; and they and their significance echoed through each celebration of the Liturgy that took place at this, the city's most sacred spot, throughout the ensuing centuries.

For St. Sophia, the imperial church, was the most important place in Constantinople for the service of the Divine Liturgy. It was here that the Patriarch officiated, and it was here that on many of the major days of the year—Christmas, Epiphany, Good Friday, Easter Monday, the Sunday after Easter, Pentecost, the Exaltation of the Cross, and several other festival days—the Emperor and the Empress, with their full court and the whole imperial suite, were present. Elaborate preparations were made for such a royal attendance. On the eve of the day in question, palatine officers known as *praepositoi* entered the Chrysotriclinos and reminded the Emperor of the service to be held on the morrow, and the Emperor gave orders for an imperial procession. The *praepositoi* then transmitted the orders to servants of the officers of the bedchamber, and to the two demarchs of the main factions. They in turn conveyed them

72

to the Domesticus of the Numera (commander of the imperial guard), to the Count of the Walls, to all military and civil officers. The Prefect of the city was also notified, so that the imperial exit to the Palace should be cleaned and the route of the procession strewn with laurel, rosemary, and other sweet-smelling flowers.

The next morning, the Emperor, clothed in a *scaramangion*, came out of his bedchamber, prayed before the image of Christ in the apse of the Chrysotriclinos, and, clad in his gold-bordered *sagum* reaching to the knees, began his procession through the Palace: he visited the chapel of our Most Blessed Lady, where he received candles and prostrated himself thrice; the chapel of the Holy Trinity, where the same procedure took place and where he venerated the holy relics; the Baptistery with the three great crosses; the church of St. Stephen, where, candles in hand, he adored the great cross of Constantine with thrice-repeated prostrations; then, donning the sacred *chlamys* and his crown, he continued through the hall of the Augusteus, where servitors stood holding gold and jewelled basins full of water, and at whose porch were presented to him some of the imperial officials, the *magistroi*, the pro-consuls, generals, the commanders of frontier forts, who stood in their proper ranks and saluted the Emperor; then through other palaces and halls—the Onopodium, where the Lord High Admiral and all the crew of the imperial galley were waiting, the Great Consistory, the Hall of the Candidatoi, the Hall of the Nineteen Couches —and so finally out through the brazen door of the Chalkê, with organ-players on either side, and where the demarch of the Blues, with the Whites behind, greeted him with the customary acclamations; through the great gate leading into the square of the Augustaeum, where the demarch of the Greens was waiting with the Red faction to acclaim him in a similar manner. A ninth-century Arabian visitor to Constantinople has described this procession as it came from the Palace and slowly made its way across the square and into St. Sophia:

(The Emperor) commands that his way from the Gate of the Palace to the Church for the common people, which is in the middle of the city, be spread with mats and upon them there be strewn aromatic plants and green foliage, and that on the right and left of his passage the walls be adorned with brocade. Then he is preceded by 10,000 elders wearing clothes of red brocade; their hair reaches their shoulders, and they wear no upper-cloak. Then behind them come 10,000 young men wearing clothes of white brocade. All go on foot, Then come 10,000 boys wearing clothes of green brocade. Then come 10,000 servants wearing clothes of brocade of the colour of the blue sky; in their hands they hold axes covered with gold. Behind them follow 5,000 chosen eunuchs wearing white Khorasanian clothes of half silk; in their hands they hold golden crosses. Then after them come 10,000 Turkish and Khorasanian pages, wearing striped breast-plates; in their hands they hold spears and shields wholly covered with gold. Then come a hundred most dignified patricians wearing clothes of coloured brocade; in their hands they have gold censers perfumed with aloes. Then come twelve chief patricians wearing clothes woven with gold; each of them holds a golden rod. Then come a hundred pages wearing clothes trimmed with borders and adorned with pearls; they carry a golden case in which is the Imperial robe for the Emperor's prayer. Then before the Emperor comes a man called al-Ruhum (?) who makes the people be silent and says, 'Be silent.' Then comes an old man holding in his hand a golden wash-basin and a golden jug adorned with pearls and rubies. Then comes the Emperor wearing his festival clothes, that is, silk clothes woven with jewels; on his head there is a crown; he wears two shoes, one of them black, the other red. The prime minister follows him. In the hand of the Emperor is a small golden box in which is a bit of earth. He goes on foot. Whenever he makes two paces, the minister says in their own language: 'μέμνησθε τοῦ θανάτου', which means in translation, 'Remember death!' When (the minister) says this to him, the Emperor pauses, opens the box, looks at the earth, kisses it, and weeps. He proceeds in this way until he reaches the gate of the Church. Then the (old) man presents the wash-basin and the jug, and the Emperor washes his hands and says to his minister: 'Truly, I am innocent of the blood of all men (cf. Matt. 27. 24)! let not God make me responsible for their blood, for I put it upon your neck.' Then he puts the clothes which he wears upon his ministers, takes the

inkstand of Pilate—that is the inkstand of the man who proclaimed himself innocent of the blood of Christ—may peace be upon him!—puts it upon the neck of the minister, and says to him: 'Rule justly as Pilate ruled justly.' Then they bring him about over the squares of Constantinople and proclaim: 'Rule justly, as the Emperor has placed you in charge of the people's affairs.'

Then the Emperor commands the Moslem captives to be brought to the Church. They look at this magnificence and power and exclaim three times: 'May God prolong the life of the Emperor for many years.' Then he orders them to be clothed with robes of honour.

Behind him are led three domesticated gray horses, upon which are golden saddles adorned with pearls and rubies and trappings of brocade in the same manner. The Emperor does not ride on them. They are introduced into the Church where bridles have been suspended. If the horse takes the bridle in its mouth, the people say: 'We have gained a victory in the land of Islam.' (Sometimes) the horse approaches, smells at the bridle, comes back, and does not draw near any more to the bridle.... [40]

At the door of the narthex of the church, the Emperor is received by the Patriarch with his suite, and, when they have greeted and embraced each other, both enter the church, proceed down the nave, and, after the customary prostration, enter into the sanctuary, where the Emperor kisses the two holy chalices offered by the Patriarch, the golden patens, and the corporal cloth. After this Emperor and Patriarch kiss the holy gilt crucifix which the Emperor then censes. Then, after the preliminary service and when the Emperor has taken up his position in the side-chapel at the east end of the south aisle, the Patriarch opens the Liturgy: 'Blessed is the Kingdom of the Father, and of the Son, and of the Holy Spirit, now and always and through all the ages.' And there unfolds the great sacred drama of the Liturgy, this drama which is not a ritual spectacle or a powerful representation of past historical events, but a reliving, through the urgent imagery of language, gesture, chant, invocation; through the developing spiritual exchange between priest, deacon, and people, of the original mystery of the Incarnation and Resurrection: that of the God who becomes man that man may become God. In the perpetual renewal of this mystery of the Liturgy the city found its justification and savoured its fulfilment: the Divine, the Eternal, the Immutable penetrated into it and transfigured it. As his envoys reported to Vladimir, Prince of Kiev, after they had been present at a celebration of this Liturgy in the great church of the Holy Wisdom: 'We know not whether we were in heaven or on earth, for surely there is no such splendour or beauty anywhere upon earth. We cannot describe it to you: only we know, that God dwells there among men, and that their service surpasses the worship of all other places. For we cannot forget that beauty.' [41]

*

Vicegerent of God on earth and holder of a supra-personal office as he was, the individual Emperor was yet mortal; and the last act in the drama of his earthly days was his death and burial. This, too, was linked through its hieratic symbolism with the drama of his divine prototype—with the death and resurrection of Christ. After the Emperor's death, his dead body, carefully embalmed, washed, anointed, and perfumed by the chief court physicians assisted by eunuchs and a whole host of chamberlains and *chitonites*, lay for several days in state on its gold 'bed of sorrow' in the Triclinos of the Nineteen Couches, a crown or diadem of chased gold on the head, the face, painted in vivid colours, exposed, the beard tended, the limbs covered in a *chlamys* of bright material woven with gold, and the high buskins of scarlet, or *campagia*, on the feet. Then, while the clerics of the Palace chanted, with low, quavering voice, the appropriate chants, the endless procession of dignitaries, courtiers, soldiers, functionaries, foreign ambassadors, patricians, barbarian chiefs carried the body to the vestibule of the Palace, the Chalkê, where the main ceremonies began. The Patriarch with the high clergy of St. Sophia, with their sweeping beards, their long hair spilling down over their shoulders, stiff in their robes of gold brocade, other priests, monks, those 'citizens of heaven clothed in the habit of angels', senators wearing the *scaramangion*, the patricians, the *magistroi*, the *spatharioi*, the *candidatoi*, the *drungaroi*, and all the other ranks of dignitaries, clothed in black, wound in slow file past the dead Emperor as he lay guarded by his white-clad eunuchs. Each at a sign from the chief eunuch prostrated himself, made the sign of the cross, cried the official words of lament, kissed the dead imperial face. Then when the vast company had filed past; when, beneath the deep vaults, in the strange shadow-cut light, the palatine crowd had gathered to the sound of the silver organs and the chants, brief and haunting, of the factions; while thick clouds of Arabian incense rose everywhere, the chief eunuch, he too clad in white, made another sign, and a hush fell, and the master of ceremonies, coming close to the dead body, called in a loud voice: 'Go from here, *basileus*; the King of kings, the Lord of Lords, summons you!' Three times he called this solemn cry, and three times all the gathered mourners and all the people of the immense city assembled in the square before the Great Church and the Palace answered with the long moans and laments of the changeless ritual. Then, while the imperial guards in dazzling costumes cleared a passage and kept back the crowd, the bier bearing the body was borne from the Palace through the city to its last resting place, the church of the Holy Apostles. Streets, squares, alleys, porticos were spread with cloth, strewn with sand and green branches. The barbarian guard, Russian, Armenian, Scandinavian, Venetian, Amalfian, or even (after the eleventh century) English, armed with double-headed axe, curved sabre, pike, and bow, lined the route where the cortège was to pass.

The church of the Holy Apostles, reconstructed by Justinian on the site of the older basilica built by Constantine the Great, was perhaps the most beautiful and celebrated of the city's churches after St. Sophia. Not only did the church itself contain the venerable relics of St. Andrew, St. Luke, and St. Paul's disciple, St. Timothy, but it was here also, in the vast courts on either side of the building, that, beginning with Constantine the Great and his mother Helena, the *basileis* and *basilissae* of Byzantium were laid to rest. For, as St. John Chrysostom (who also had his tomb there, with that of other Patriarchs) wrote, it was fitting for the Emperor to have the great honour of being laid in the vestibule of those fishermen, the Apostles, since *what the gatekeepers of palaces are to the sovereign, the Emperors are to the fishermen in their place of burial. For the latter* (the Apostles) *are the masters who dwell within the place; and the former* (the Emperors), *like neighbours living nearby, are happy to have the gate of the courtyard entrusted to their care, so that from these places they may show unbelievers that at the time of resurrection the fishermen enjoy greater prominence.* Here, then, in huge silver-sheeted, stone-encrusted sarcophagi, dazzling where the sun's ray struck, lay the mortal remains of God's terrestrial vicars, the valiant and the timid, those whose life had been one long struggle and those who had slowly decayed within the Palace walls: Constantine the Great, Theodosius and his degenerate sons; the 'infamous and execrable' Julian, that hallucinated sophist whose cylindrical tomb the Orthodox had respected where they had broken open that of the iconoclast Constantine Copronymus and had scattered his dust to the winds; Justinian, enclosed in the green marble of Hierapolis, his ephemeral conquests and theatrical magnificence still able to rouse the imagination of Dante:

> *Cesare fui, e son Giustiniano....*
> *A Dio per grazia piacque d'inspirarmi*
> *L'alto lavoro....*

Heraclius, a second Alexander to his contemporaries, brilliant meteor so soon spent: all this august assembly of imperial corpses housed in their tombs of carved porphyry, of rich and strange granites, which were to be profaned and pillaged first by the Emperor Alexis Angelus, who used their treasure to purchase peace from the Latin crusaders; then by these same crusaders in the unbridled rapacity of their destruction on the nights of 13 and 14 April 1204; then finally by the unleashed troops of Mahomet II who on those days and nights following 29 May 1453 spent fourteen hours breaking them with blows from iron bars, their shattered fragments to end up in a lime-kiln or in the wall of some humble Turkish house. 'Enter into your rest, *basileus;* the King of kings, the Lord of Lords, summons you!' Again here, at this church of the Holy Apostles, encircled by the gigantic tombs, the cry of the master of ceremonies rang out as the long sacred chants quivered to a halt: 'Take the crown from the head!' And the metal crown was removed, and in its place was set a simple purple diadem; and the body of the mystic Caesar, his part in the great drama done, was laid to rest among his peers.

Cross from a Byzantine
reliquary made of ivory.

Illustration opposite: Byzantine altar-hanging with the entombment of Christ, from the twelfth century, in the cathedral treasury of St. Mark at Venice.

The New Jerusalem

If of those two aspects of the symbolism of the dome which we noted, the one—that of the 'Christos Basileus', the universal Monarch—had its earthly counterpart in and lent support to the office of the God-appointed Emperor and hence to the whole elaboration of Constantinople as the New Rome, the other—that linked with the transfiguration and the coming of the Kingdom of God—was reflected in the city's character as the New Jerusalem. 'And I John saw the holy city, new Jerusalem, coming down from God out of heaven, prepared as a bride adorned for her husband. And I heard a great voice out of heaven saying, Behold, the tabernacle of God is with men, and he will dwell with them, and be their God.' [42] These words of St. John had their literal significance for the Byzantines. For the symbolism which applied first of all to the great church of St. Sophia—that of the church as the material and animated house of the Logos, the temple of his own flesh—applied also by extension to Constantinople as a whole: not the church alone, but the city as a whole was to be the dwelling-place of the Divinity, the tabernacle of God; was to be the radiant image of the heavenly kingdom, of the new Jerusalem, adorned like a bride for her husband, in which God was to dwell.

This in its turn meant something else. For if Constantinople was to be the tabernacle of God, in this respect also it was to imitate the character of the church, that like the church it was visibly to perpetuate the role of the Mother of God. For the Queen of Heaven was also the Queen of the new Jerusalem; and if Constantinople was to be the image of this divine city, it could by analogy claim as its own mistress the Queen of Heaven, Mary the All Holy. For Christ's earthly tabernacle was no less than this exalted Lady, and so it could be no less than her also, the inviolable mediator of the king of kings, who was the indwelling reality, the succour and protectress, of Constantinople: *It was needful that she who had formed herself beautifully with spiritual comeliness should appear as a chosen bride, fitting for the heavenly Bridegroom. It was needful that she who with her virtuous ways, as with stars, had likened herself to the heavens, should be revealed to all the faithful as giving rise to the sun of righteousness. It was needful that she who had dyed herself once with the dye of her virginal blood should serve as the purple of the universal Emperor.... The living and heavenly oven is being forged on earth, wherein the Creator of our clay, having baked the first-fruits with a divine fire and burnt up the crop of tares, makes unto Himself a bread of wholly pure flour. But what is one to say, what would one not experience, sailing over the high sea of the Virgin's gifts and achievements? One fears and rejoices, one is calm and excited, one is hushed again and cries out, one cowers and expands, sometimes drawn by fear, sometimes by love.* [43] It was in such terms as these, uttered by the Constantinopolitan Patriarch Photius, that the Byzantines thought of the Mother of God, the Queen of Heaven. It was in such terms as these also that, by virtue of an ineluctable transference and interpenetration of symbolic role and function, they thought of their city, the Queen of Cities, as they called it, fitting it out in that indescribable richness of apparel which we have partially described not merely for display but to be worthy of the heavenly Bridegroom: *And the city was pure gold, like unto clear glass. And the foundations of the wall of the city were garnished with all manner of precious stone. The first foundation was jasper; the second, sapphire; the third, a chalcedony; the fourth, an emerald; the fifth, sardonyx; the sixth, sardius; the seventh, chrysolyte; the eighth, beryl; the ninth, a topaz; the tenth, a chrysoprasus; the eleventh, a jacinth; the twelfth, an amethyst. And the twelve gates were twelve pearls; every several gate was of one pearl: and the street of the city was pure gold, as it were transparent glass.* [44] This was the model of whose splendour Constantinople had to be the image.

Illustration opposite: The Blessed Virgin of Vladimir, the most famous miraculous icon in Russia; it was probably painted in Constantinople in the twelfth century, and is now in the Tretiakov Gallery in Moscow. The later over-painting on the faces has been removed, so that the original Byzantine painting can be seen.

It was because of this, because the Byzantines had by all means to strengthen the likeness of their city to the celestial model, that they multiplied throughout its length and breadth the visible tokens of this assimilation. And this meant first of all that they multiplied the visible tokens of the indwelling presence of her who was both the model's and the city's Queen, of her who not only was God's Mother but also had full confidence of intercession in the court of Heaven. More sanctuaries—and these were numberless—were dedicated to her than to anyone else. 'You will not find any public place or imperial dwelling, no reputable inn or private house of those in authority where there is not a church or an oratory of the Mother of God.' [45] Of these sanctuaries, 'head and metropolis' was the church at Blachernae, at the north-west extremity of the landward walls. Here was kept one of the most precious of all the city's relics, its veritable Palladium, the Virgin's robe. The robe had been brought to Constantinople in the time of Leo I the Great (457–474) and his wife Verina by two of the city's inhabitants, the patricians Galbius and Candidus from Palestine. When they returned to the capital with the relic, they said nothing about it either to Emperor or Empress or to the Patriarch, for they were afraid that their treasure would be taken from them. Instead, with the Virgin's blessing, they built a church, which they dedicated to St. Peter and St. Mark in order to preserve the secret, and they placed the robe in this church, providing also for hymns to be sung continually and for lights to burn continually and for the church to be filled continually with sweet odours. But the Virgin again intervened: she wanted the secret of Galbius and Candidus to be known to all, and she moved them to disclose it. There was then great rejoicing and the finders of the robe were publicly honoured, and Leo and Verina built in the quarter of Blachernae an imperial church, which they dedicated to the Virgin and where they placed the robe in a reliquary of silver and gold. And 'that church, it might be said, contains the whole mystagogia—the secret and the power of Christians. Here in truth all sickness, all grief, and all distress are cured, all joy and rejoicing and the hope for better things is here confirmed'. [46]

It was also the sanctuary at Blachernae that held the miraculous icon of the Virgin to which one went to pray for a favour secretly desired. The icon was hidden by a veil which covered it completely. At certain moments the veil opened, disclosing the icon, then again it miraculously shut. And it was at Blachernae too that, in the reign of Leo the Wise, St. Andrew the Fool for Christ saw, on Christmas night, the Virgin weep over her people and then turn and stretch over them the protecting veil of her interceding tears. [47]

Other sanctuaries to the Mother of God possessed either some relic or some icon that compelled an almost equal veneration. Most famous was perhaps that situated not far from St. Sophia, in the quarter of the coppersmiths and called for that reason the church of Our Lady of the Chalcopratia. It was here that had been placed the box containing the Virgin's girdle, a relic that had produced a host of miracles. It was here also that was kept that icon, known as the 'Roman Mary', which had been launched on the seas by the Patriarch in order to save it from destruction at the hands of the iconoclast Emperor Leo III. Sailing upright on the sea for one night and one day, the icon was said to have reached old Rome, where it had been placed by the Pope in a church dedicated to St. Peter. But time passed, Orthodoxy triumphed over the iconoclasts, and a longing came upon the icon to return to the city to which it belonged. It struggled to free itself from its fittings, rattled, and shook. The people in the church were alarmed. They stopped their hymns and, full of foreboding, took up the invocation of the *kyrie eleison*. Then the icon tore itself loose and made its way down to the Tiber and so out into the open sea. In one day and one night it again journeyed upright to its beloved city, where, rescued from the waters by the faithful, it was hung in the church of the Chalcopratia. In yet another sanctuary, that of Our Lady Hodigitria (the Guide), was another of the city's most powerful supports, the icon of the Virgin that the Emperors took with them when they went to war or which was carried round the walls when the enemy menaced the city.

The Blessed Virgin of the Veil, after a sixteenth-century icon from Novgorod. St. Andrew, 'the Fool for Christ', who can be recognized in the half-naked figure at the bottom, right, points out to his disciple Epiphanios the Blessed Virgin, as she spreads out her veil, which is held up by two angels, over the congregation in the church at Blachernae. In the foreground is the ambo with St. Romanos the Melodist, who immediately sings the Christmas Kontakion in honour of the Mother of God.

For it was Mary the Mother of God who saved the city from the many perils with which through the centuries it was threatened. Whether it was from the Avars, or the Arabs, or the Russians, or the Turks, it was always the same: it was through the robe, the girdle, the icon, the intercession of the Blessed Virgin that deliverance came. It was after the people had taken refuge with the Virgin and after the Patriarch Sergius, in the absence of the Emperor, had taken charge that, in 626, the assaults of the Avars were miraculously repulsed from the walls and the Avar fleet was blown on to the shores in the Blachernae quarter. And it was said that it was on this night that the people of Constantinople, who were so dear to God, gathered in the church of Our Lady at Blachernae and sang that most magnificent of all Christian hymns, the Hymn of the Annunciation or the Akathistos Hymn, 'standing and without respite during the whole night, as a thanksgiving to the Mother of God, as she had kept watch over them and with her great might had achieved the monument of victory over the enemies':

An angel of the first rank was sent from heaven to say to the Mother of God: 'Hail'; and seeing you, Lord, become corporeal at the incorporeal voice, he was amazed and stood still and cried out to her: 'Hail, you through whom joy shall shine forth. Hail, you through whom the curse will be lifted. Hail, recalling of the fallen Adam. Hail, release of the tears of Eve. Hail, height hard to scale for human minds. Hail, depth hard to behold even for the eyes of Angels. Hail, because you are the throne of the king. Hail, because you bear the Bearer of all. Hail, star manifesting the Sun. Hail, womb of the divine Incarnation. Hail, through whom creation is renewed. Hail, through whom the Creator is childed. Hail, unbrided Bride.' [48]

It was through the Mother of God again that the city was saved from the Russians in 860, *at the time when, denuded of all help, and deprived of human alliance,* as a contemporary witness, the Patriarch Photius, put it, *we were spiritually led on by holding fast to our hopes in the Mother of the Logos, our God, urging her to implore her Son, invoking her for the expiation of our sins, her intercession for our salvation, her protection as an impregnable wall for us, begging her to break the boldness of the barbarians, her to crush their insolence, her to defend the despairing people and fight for her own flock. When, moreover, as the whole city was carrying with me her robe for the repulse of the besiegers and the protection of the besieged, we offered freely our prayers and performed the litany, thereupon with ineffable compassion she spoke out in motherly intercession: God was moved. His anger was averted, and the Lord took pity on his inheritance. Truly,* Photius continues, *is this most holy garment the robe of God's Mother! It embraced the walls, and the foes inexplicably showed their backs; the city put it around itself, and the camp of the enemy was broken up as at a signal; the city bedecked itself with it, and the enemy were deprived of the hopes which bore them on. For immediately as the Virgin's robe went round the walls, the barbarians gave up the siege and broke camp, while we were delivered from impending capture and were granted unexpected salvation.* [49]

And, in a most vivid piece of writing, a late historiographer of Constantinople describes how in 1422, on the day on which the astrologers of Persia had predicted that the city must fall and when the Turks were in sight of victory, they suddenly saw a woman wearing violet-coloured robes walking fearless on the ramparts; and it was she who repulsed the powers of the stars and the arts of the astrologers. For seeing her, darkness and confusion and terror and fear entered the souls of all the Turks, and they thought no more of war but only of how to flee; and it was by the power and art of this lady that the city was again delivered. [50]

So through relics, through icons, through the numberless churches, was the city's Protectress worshipped, as well as through the endless cycle of commemorative rites that filled the calendar, when Emperor and court and people would go in procession to the sanctuary at which the particular feast was to be celebrated and there would listen to the praises of their all-victorious leader, praises like those in the following extract from a homily delivered on the dedication-day of one of her churches by the Patriarch Germanos:

The Blessed Virgin in the attitude of prayer. Painted in Russia in the 12th or 13th century after the original picture of the Mother of God at Blachernae. Tretiakov Gallery, Moscow.

O most holy, good, and compassionate Lady, comfort of Christians, warmest consolation of the afflicted, most ready refuge of sinners, do not leave us orphans of your protection. For if you abandon us, where then can we turn? And what then shall we become, O most holy Mother of God, breath and life of Christians? For as breathing is proof of our body's vital energy, so your most holy name ceaselessly proffered on the lips of your servants at all times and in all places and circumstances, does not prove but provides life and joyousness and help. Cover us with the wings of your goodness. Guard us with your intercessions. Grant us, unshamed hope of Christians, eternal life. For we, poor in divine works and ways, exclaim when we see the wealth of benefits granted to us through you: 'the earth is full of the Lord's mercy'. We, driven out from God in the multitude of our sins, through you have sought and found God, and having found him have been saved. Greatly therefore you assist our salvation, Mother of God, and we have no need of other interceder before God. Knowing this, having indeed learnt it by experience from the many times we have besought you, our warmest protection, profusely we receive the granting of our requests, and now again we, your people, your inheritance, your flock, beautified by the election of your Son, resort to you. Truly there is no limit to your majesty; there is no measure of your care; your benefits are without number. No one is saved but through you, most holy one. No one is freed from affliction but through you, unblemished one. No one, O most Pure, is granted gifts but through you. O most August, no one has found mercy in grace but through you. Who then will not bless you? Who will not magnify you?—if not according to your worth, at least most readily: you who are glorified; you who are blessed; you who greatly and wonderfully receive majesty from your Son and God. Wherefore all generations shall honour you....

But O vase from which we, consumed with affliction, drink the manna of relief; table from which we, the famished, are filled with the bread of life; lampstand from which we who are in darkness are illumined by great light: if from God you have the praise that is due and fitting, do not reject our unworthy praise, ardently brought before you. Do not reject, all-hymned one, hymns fervently offered from our unclean lips. Do not despise the supplicatory word of an unworthy tongue. But measuring the ardour, O God-glorified, grant us forgiveness of sins, enjoyment of eternal life, and deliverance from all hurt. Look with favour, Mother of God, from this your holy dwelling on your faithful congregation gathered about you, on those who have enriched you with the epithets of Lady and Protectress and Mistress, and who have come together to hymn you with all their soul; and having visited them with your divine care, take from them every misfortune and affliction of all sickness, all hurt; shield them from all abuse; fill them with all joy, all healing, all grace; and in the coming of your Son our compassionate God, when we are all presented for judgement, lead us, as having maternal fearlessness and influence, with your strong arm away from the eternal fire, making us worthy of eternal blessings: through the grace and compassion of our Lord Jesus Christ, to whom you gave birth and to whom be the glory and the power, now and through all the ages. Amen. [51]

*

The Mother of God was not the only, even if she was the chief, protector of Constantinople. For if the Mother of God is *par excellence* the temple in which the mysterious union of the divine and human natures takes place; if it is she above all who has given her blood and flesh to form the body of the incarnate Logos, the body and blood of the saint and holy man have also received the deifying grace of the Divine, have also become bearers of the Spirit, hypostatically united to God; and this grace has spilled over into those material objects with which the saint or holy man has come into contact. And if God is, in the words of the Liturgy, at rest among his saints, and it is this presence of the Divinity among his saints that constitutes his Kingdom, the heavenly Jerusalem, it follows that the earthly city, this new Jerusalem, image of the Kingdom, must imitate its prototype even in this, that within its walls should be gathered sanctified, consecrated objects of saintliness in which the Divinity is at rest. *We venerate the created things by which and in which God has achieved our salvation*, wrote St. John of Damascus. *It is thus that I venerate and*

Centre-piece of the lid of a cross-reliquary *(staurothêkê)* in the Cathedral treasury of Limburg an der Lahn. This case for a relic of the true cross, of silver gilt with coloured enamel, comes from Constantinople and was made at the end of the tenth century.

that I salute Mount Sinai, Nazareth, Bethlehem, the Grotto, Calvary, the wood of the holy Cross, the sepulchre, Mount Sion, the Mount of Olives, the Garden of Gethsemane, and so on. I venerate each temple of God and every place where God's name is invoked; and I do not venerate them for themselves, but because they are the vessels of the action of God, because God has chosen them in order to fulfil our life. It is in this way that I venerate and salute angels, men, and all matter which serves for my salvation in the action of God. In saluting and venerating the relics of sanctity, in bowing down before those objects that have been intimately connected with

Christ, the saints, the martyrs, and which are still penetrated by their influence, the inhabitant of the earthly city is brought into the presence, made of the company of the inhabitants of the heavenly city; becomes therefore himself in some measure a citizen of the Kingdom, chosen and exalted by the inscrutable majesty of God.

Thus through a formal extension of the city's original symbolic role supported by the authority of the Church Fathers, Constantinople became the abode of countless relics gathered from the whole Christian world: became in fact one enormous reliquary. Here, in one of the palatine sanctuaries, was the right hand of St. Stephen, the first martyr; here, also in a palatine sanctuary, was that portrait of himself, 'not made with hands', which Christ had sent to Abgar, king of Edessa, as well as the autographed letter that he had sent with it; here too was the lance with which Christ had been pierced on the Cross, and the Crown of Thorns, and one of the holy nails, and the stone of the Tomb; in yet a third palatine sanctuary lay parts of the headdress and belt of the Prophet Elijah; elsewhere, in the church of the Holy Apostles, alongside whose walls lay the great imperial tombs, reposed the relics of the Apostles St. Luke and St. Andrew, and of St. Paul's disciple Timothy, while before the altar stood the column of Christ's flagellation; in a church dedicated to him was the head of John the Baptist; and so on: in the endless churches, sanctuaries, shrines, encased in their reliquaries of gold and silver, ornamented with precious stones, often wrapped in a cloth of silk, lay the countless relics which piety, love, and devotion had brought from all the provinces of the Empire into the capital, miraculous sources of protection and healing, witness and gage of the city's supernatural destiny. And, as was fitting, nowhere was the display of relics more magnificent than in the great church of St. Sophia. A Russian pilgrim, Antony of Novgorod, who visited the city in 1200, a few years before its sack by the Latin crusaders, has left a description of his visit to this church and of the relics he saw there:

I, Antonius, Archbishop of Novgorod, an unworthy and humble sinner, by the grace of God and by the help of St. Sophia, who is the Wisdom of the Eternal Word, reached in safety the imperial city, and entered the great Catholic and Apostolic Church. We first worshipped St. Sophia, kissing the two slabs of the Lord's sepulchre. Furthermore we saw the seals, and the figure of the Mother of God, nursing Christ. This image a Jew at Jerusalem pierced in the neck with a knife, and blood flowed forth. The blood of the image, all dried up, we saw in the smaller sanctuary.

In the sanctuary of S. Sophia is the blood of the holy martyr Pantaleon with milk, placed in a reliquary like a little branch or bough, yet without their having mixed. Besides that there is his head, and the head of the Apostle Quadratus, and many relics of other saints: the heads of Hermolaus and Stratonicus; the arm of Germanos, which is laid on those who are to be ordained Patriarchs; the image of the Virgin which Germanos sent in a boat to Rome by sea; and the small marble table on which Christ celebrated His Supper with the disciples, as well as His swaddling clothes and the golden Vessels, which the Magi brought with their offerings.

There is a large gold paten for the mass, given to the Patriarch by Olga, a Russian princess, when she came to the imperial city to be baptized. In this paten there is a precious stone which displays the image of Christ, and the seal-impressions from this are used as charms; but on the upper side the disc is adorned with pearls.

In the sanctuary is likewise preserved the real chariot of Constantine and Helena, made of silver; there are gold plates, enriched with pearls and little jewels, and numerous others of silver, which are used for the services on Sundays and feast days: there is water also in the sanctuary coming out of a well by pipes.

Outside the smaller sanctuary is erected the 'Crux Mensuralis', which shows the height of Christ when on earth; and behind that cross is buried Anna, who gave her house to St. Sophia, where now is the smaller sanctuary, and she is buried near. And near this same smaller sanctuary are the figures of the holy women and of the Virgin Mother holding Christ, and shedding tears which fall on the eyes of Christ. They give of the water of the sanctuary for the blessing of the world.

In the same part is the chapel of St. Peter the Apostle, where St. Theophania is buried. She was the guardian of the keys of St. Sophia, which people used to kiss. There is also suspended the carpet of St. Nicholas. The iron chains of St. Peter are kept there in a gold chest; during the feast of 'St. Peter's Chains' the Emperor, the Patriarch, and all the congregation kiss them. Near by, in another chapel, is also shown the crystal of the ancient ambo, destroyed when the dome fell.

By the side of (the images of) the holy women is the tomb of the son of St. Athenogenius.... There are no other tombs in St. Sophia except that, and a lamp hangs in front of it, which once fell, full of oil, without being broken. The place is inclosed by a wooden screen, and the people are not allowed to enter.

When one turns towards the gate one sees at the side the column of St. Gregory the Miracle-Worker, all covered with bronze plates. St. Gregory appeared near this column, and the people kiss it, and rub their breasts and shoulders against it to be cured of their pains; there is also the image of St. Gregory. On his feast day the Patriarch brings his relics to this column. And there placed above a platform is a great figure of the Saviour in mosaic; it lacks the little finger of the right hand. When it was finished, the artist looked at it and said, 'Lord, I have made thee as if alive'. Then a voice coming from the picture said, 'When hast thou seen me?' The artist was struck dumb and died, and the finger was not finished, but was made in silver-gilt.

Above the gate is depicted on a large panel the Emperor Leo the Wise, and in front of it is a precious stone, which illuminates St. Sophia at night-time. This same Emperor Leo took a certain writing from Babylon, which was found in the tomb of the Prophet Daniel. It was copied, and on it were written the names of the Greek Emperors. At the royal gate is a bronze romanistum or bolt by which the door is closed. Men and women are brought to it, and if they have drunk serpent poison or any other poison, they cannot remove the bolt from the mouth, until all the evil of the disease has trickled away with the saliva.

By the great altar on the left is the place where the angel of the Lord appeared to the boy who was guarding the workmen's tools, and said, 'I will not leave this spot as long as St. Sophia shall remain.' Three figures are shown in this place, for the angels are painted there; and a multitude of people come there to pray to God. Not far from there is the place where they boil the holy oil, burning underneath it old icons, whose features one can no longer trace. With this oil they anoint children at baptism. Above the sanctuary there rises in the air a great hollow vault covered with gold. In the sanctuary are eighty candelabra of silver for use on feast days, which occupy the first place, besides numberless silver candelabra with many golden apples.

Above the great altar in the middle is hung the crown of the Emperor Constantine, set with precious stones and pearls. Below it is a golden cross, which overhangs a golden dove. The crowns of the other Emperors are hung around the ciborium, which is entirely made of silver and gold. Thus the altar pillars and the sanctuary and the bema are built of gold and silver, ingeniously made, and very costly. From the same ciborium hang thirty smaller crowns, as a remembrance to Christians of the pieces of money of Judas.... When Jerusalem was taken by Titus many sacred vessels and curtains were brought to (New) Rome with the royal treasures and given to the church of St. Sophia. In St. Sophia also are preserved the tables of the Law, as well as the Ark and manna. The subdeacons, when they sing 'Alleluia' in the ambo, hold in their hands tablets like those of Moses. During the procession of the Holy Sacrament the eunuchs begin to sing, and then the subdeacons, and then a monk chants alone. Then many priests and deacons carry the Holy Sacrament in procession; at this time all the people not only below, but also in the galleries, weep in great humility. What then ought to be the fear and humility of the bishops, the priests, and the deacons in this holy service?

How magnificent are the gold and silver chalices, garnished with precious stones and pearls! When the splendid chest, called Jerusalem, is brought out with the flabella, there rises among the people a great groaning and weeping.... But here is a wonderful miracle, which we saw in St. Sophia. Behind the altar of the larger sanctuary is a gold cross, higher than two men, set with precious stones and pearls. There hangs before it another gold cross a cubit and a half long, with three gold lamps, which hang from as many gold arms (the fourth is now lost). These

Illustration opposite: Book-cover of silver, decorated with enamel, of a Byzantine gospel-book of the tenth or eleventh century in the Cathedral treasury of St. Mark at Venice.

89

lamps, the arms or branches, and the cross, were made by the great Emperor Justinian who built St. Sophia. By virtue of the Holy Spirit the small cross with the lamps ascended above the big cross, and again slowly came down again without going out. This miracle took place after matins, before the beginning of the mass: the priests who were in the sanctuary saw it, and all the people in the church who saw it cried with fear and joy, 'God in His mercy has visited us'....

At St. Sophia on the right near the sanctuary is a piece of red marble, on which they place a golden throne; on this throne the Emperor is crowned. This place was surrounded by bronze closures to prevent people walking on it; but the people kiss it. At this place the Holy Virgin prayed to her Son, our Lord, on behalf of all Christians; a priest who was guarding the church at night saw her. On the same side is also the grand icon of St. Boris and St. Gleb, which artists copy. When officiating, the Patriarch holds it high up in the tribune.

In the chapel behind the altar are affixed to the wall the upper slab of the Lord's sepulchre, the hammer, the gimlet, and the saw, with which the Cross of the Lord was made; also the iron chain which was hung to the gate of St. Peter's prison, and the wood of the Cross which Christ's neck touched. This is inserted in a reliquary in the form of a cross. In this chapel above the door is painted St. Stephen, protomartyr, and a lamp is hung before him; when anyone has bad eyes, they put round his head the rope by which this lamp is hung, and his eyes are healed.

There is also the figure of Christ whose neck the Jew struck, and the bronze trumpet of Joshua, who took Jericho, and the marble mouth of the well of Samaria. Near it Christ said to the woman, 'Give me to drink'; the well mouth has been cut in half, and the Samaritans still draw water (from the other half).[52]

We may see in the veneration of sacred relics nothing more than pious excess or vain superstition, or at most a gesture of respect for the holy dead. But for the Byzantines this veneration implied something more significant. It implied a communion with a reality that has become deiform; with a past transfigured by its sanctity into an eternal here and now. For because penetrated with something of the divine power of those holy personages to which they belong, these relics represent so many openings into time of the trans-temporal glory of the Kingdom of God: shafts of illumination breaking through the obscurity of human existence as the rays of the sun broke through the corona of windows in the dome of St. Sophia to light the congregation standing on the pavement below. It was because of this vision maintained through such a communion of the saints that Constantinople could be called, as it was called, 'the eye of the faith of the Christians'.[53]

*

The promise and hope of this vision were also the cornerstones of the activity of those who more than others made saintliness the dominating study of their own lives: the monks of the many monasteries of Constantinople. For with the monks—or with those monks whose practice of their profession was equal to its demand—the effort towards transcendence, towards the realization of a *beyond* whose reality is *hic et nunc*, was all-absorbing and continuous, and implied a total break with the limitations of the purely human state as with the ties and obligations of the earthly city to which this state was attached. This is not to say that of the thousands of monks—and nuns—that throughout its history flooded the imperial capital many were not more worldly than the lay citizen, or that ignorance, greed, concern for material comforts never found a place within the monastic walls: criticism, often most bitter, of monks is to be found throughout the Byzantine period in the writings of ecclesiastic and layman alike. But, first, the monastic life in the full sense of the word was regarded as the highest form of life a man could live on earth, and, second, the traditions of this life were maintained unbroken at the highest level while Constantinople endured as a Christian city. So that the part played by monasticism in forging and preserving that sense of the sacred, that allegiance to realities of a superhuman order, by virtue of which the city could claim to be the spiritual centre of a civilization, was immense. Here that preoccupation with the imminence of the transfiguration, the immanence of the Heavenly Jerusalem, which characterizes so many aspects of the city's life, was direct and ceaseless. The demands made, in terms of renunciation and self-sacrifice, so that it could be direct and ceaseless, were correspondingly immense, no less than total turning away and detachment from the world and its concerns. 'Do not acquire any of this world's goods, nor hoard up privately for yourself to the value of one piece of silver', wrote one of the great figures of Christian monasticism, St. Theodore, Abbot of the Monastery of Stoudios in Constantinople, to one of his pupils who was in his turn about to become an Abbot. And he continues:

Be without distraction in heart and soul in your care and your thought for those who have been entrusted to you by God, and have become your spiritual sons and brothers; and do not look aside to those formerly belonging to you according to the flesh, whether kinsfolk, or friends, or companions. Do not spend the property of your monastery, in life or death, by way of gift or legacy, to any such kinsfolk or friends. For you are not of the world, neither have you part in the world. Except that if any of your people come out of ordinary life to join our rule, you must care for them according to the example of the Holy Fathers. Do not obtain any slave, nor use in your private service or in that of the monastery over which you preside, or in the fields, man who was made in the image of God. For such an indulgence is only for those who live in the world. For you yourself should be as a servant to the brethren like-minded with you, at least in intention, even if in outward appearance you are reckoned to be master and teacher. Have no animal of the female sex in domestic use (for you have renounced the female sex altogether), whether in house or fields, since none of the Holy Fathers had such, nor does nature require them. Do not be driven by horses and mules without necessity, but go on foot in imitation of Christ. But if there is need let your beast be the foal of an ass. Use all care that all things in the brotherhood be common and not distributed, and let nothing, not even a needle, belong to any one in particular. Let your body and your spirit, to say nothing of your goods, be ever divided in equality of love among all your spiritual children and brethren.... Do not have any choice or costly garment, except for priestly functions. But follow the Fathers in being shod and clad in humility. Be not delicate in food, in private expenditure, or in hospitality; for this belongs to the portion of those who take their joy in the present life. Do not lay up money in your monastery; but things of all kinds, beyond what is needed, give to the poor at the entrance of your court; for so did the Holy Fathers.... Do nothing, carry out nothing, according to your own judgement, in any matter whatever, in journeying, buying or selling, receiving or rejecting a brother, or in any change of office or in anything material, or in regard to spiritual failings, without the counsel of those who stand first in knowledge and piety, one, two, three, or more, according to circumstances, as the Fathers have directed. These commands, and all others that you have received, keep and maintain, that it may be well with you, and that you may have prosperity in the Lord all the days of your life: But let anything to the contrary be far from you in speech and thought. [54]

The monastery of Stoudios was in fact one of the outstanding of the city's monasteries, and St. Theodore was one of its outstanding Abbots. The monastery was said to have been founded originally in 454 by a certain Stoudios, a Consul in Rome, and its church was dedicated to St. John the Baptist in 462 or 463. At first it had not been intended as a monastic establishment, but it was shortly after its erection occupied by a group of monks known as Akoimetoi (the Sleepless), not because they never slept but because they maintained a ceaseless round of psalmody and prayer. Essentially a contemplative community, and extremely zealous in the cause of Orthodox doctrine (it was they who refused to admit an Abbot unless the consecrating bishop first anathematized the opponents of the Chalcedonian decrees), they were exiled from Constantinople at the time of the Iconoclast controversy (they were, in common with the monastic element in general, strong supporters of the worship of icons), and it was when, sadly depleted in number, they returned to the city after the first restoration of icons by the Empress Irene in 787, that Theodore was appointed their Abbot. Under his direction the monastery, reorganized, became itself a miniature city with its own craftsmen, builders, tailors, gardeners, and its fine school of calligraphists and hymnologers. The rule was strict, the spiritual direction intense. Of Theodore himself there remains a whole series of short discourses addressed to his monks, terse, pointed, uncompromising. Often their point of departure is some local event or accident—the arrival of a messenger from the court, an ailment in Theodore's foot, a market day, the vintage, or, as in the case of the following discourse, the time of sowing:

The time has come for the sowing of earthly seed, of corn and of other things, he begins an exhortation to the pursuit of the spiritual harvest. *We see men going forth to work from the end to the beginning of the night, taking all care that they may sow what is best and most productive, that the needs of the body may be supplied. And shall we, the husbandmen of spiritual seed, sleep our time away, and neglect to sow what we should? How then should we bear everlasting hunger? What excuse can we give for our idleness? Let us awake, then, and sow more zealously and more plentifully than the sowers of natural seed! For he that soweth sparingly shall reap sparingly, and he that soweth in blessing shall reap blessings. What do we sow? Petitions, prayers, supplications, thanksgivings, faith, hope, love. These are the seeds of piety, and by them the soul is nourished. With the natural seed the husbandman can only be patient, awaiting the early and the latter rain. But of our seed we are masters to cause rain and dew—our weeping and contrition—at our will, and as much as pleases us. Since this is within our choice, I beseech you, brethren, let us also sow much and let us water very much, and let us increase the fruits of righteousness that when the spiritual harvest of the unseen world shall come, we may fill our hands and our laps with sheaves, and may cry aloud: 'The blessing of the Lord is upon us. We have blessed you out of the house of the Lord. Thou shalt eat the labours of thy hands. Thou art blessed, and it shall be well with thee....' Only let us walk worthy of the Gospel, having our citizenship in heaven. For we are strangers and sojourners upon earth. We have no part nor lot therein. For who, coming from eternity, has remained in the world, that he might inherit anything? Have not all who have come in gone out as from a strange land? For this is but a place of sojourning. Our true home and heritage and abiding-place is in the world to come. May we come thither and be accounted worthy to inherit with all the saints the kingdom of Heaven in Christ Jesus our Lord, to whom be the glory and the power with the Father and the Holy Spirit now and through all the ages. Amen.*[55]

What the spiritual direction at this monastery could mean for one who would hit the mark of his calling we may learn from the biography of another Stoudite monk, St. Symeon the New Theologian. Son of a wealthy Paphlagonian family and destined for high service at court, he yet persevered in his early desire to become a monk, and, under the guidance of his confessor and spiritual father, he entered the monastery of Stoudios. His biographer, Nicetas Stethatos, gives an account of his entry into the monastery:

The next day the courageous youth presented himself to the superior (Peter was the name of him who at this time directed the great flock of the Stoudites), and having put down the two pounds of gold for the monastery he donned the sack of the exercise of the virtues. As there was no cell empty in which the young man could stay, the Abbot entrusted him to this noble father: both of them thought this was best in view of Symeon's young age. The father, receiving him whom he had nourished from early childhood with the teaching of the Word, told him to stay under the stairs of his cell, and there to meditate on the narrow way; there was there in fact a kind of tomb-like cell in which, in spite of its extreme narrowness, he entered and slept. Thus he began to exercise himself in still further struggles for virtue, while his spiritual father taught him the rules of this art. The father said to him: 'See, my child, if you wish to be saved and to escape the ambushes of the Evil One, pay attention only to yourself and do not enter into conversation with any of those of the holy gathering here, nor go from cell to cell, but be a stranger and withdrawn from every human being, having in mind your sins and considering the eternal punishments, keeping your mind from wandering among external things; for you will find great profit if you maintain this.

Hearing these things as though from the mouth of God, Symeon kept them without fault. But wishing to furnish him with further crowns, the father who exercised him imposed on him the most mean services in his cell.

One half of a double
icon in mosaic from
Constantinople,
depicting: the Entry
into Jerusalem; the
Crucifixion; the Des-
cent into Hell; the
Ascension of Christ;
the Pentecost; and
the Dormition of
the B.V.M. First half
of the fourteenth
century. Florence,
Museo dell'Opera del
Duomo.

93

Symeon, however, once and for all subjecting himself to the Elder, readily carried out everything, considering himself a slave and a stranger, being even prepared to throw himself into a burning furnace or into the depths of the sea if so he were ordered, and this eagerly and with joy. Performing thus all the most dishonourable services and striving greatly, he disregarded neither fasts nor vigils, but knowing the profit to be derived from them he entered into them unconstrainedly. The Elder, wishing to break his self-will, frequently commanded him to do the opposite to all this, compelling him to eat and to sleep. This made Symeon extremely sorrowful, but he bore all the various exercises, for the divine Elder in his wisdom now made him savour humiliations and toil, now offered him honour and respite; and from both he gained his reward, in opposing his will. Exercised in this way by the father, and thus moulded to the best shape, Symeon so grew in faith and reverence for the father, that he was careful to tread the ground where the father's foot had trod and he regarded every place in which he saw him standing and praying as the holy of holies, and he prostrated himself before it and kissed it, and from it he wiped with his hands the tears of his master and carried them to his head and his heart as a balm; and he considered himself altogether unworthy of touching one of his garments. [56]

Such a complete recognition and veneration of God's superior gifts and graces in another, and the implications of this, might be rare. But it corresponded to an objective estimate of the value of the saint or holy man. For he was one who, breaking through the barrier set by the forces of negation and illusion between man and God, and fusing the human and divine natures once more in vital conjunction, gave fullest evidence of that participation in the life of the Spirit by which human existence might be crowned. Hence the regard in which he was held was unrivalled, even by that in which the Emperor was held. The Emperor might be God's elect. The saint or holy man was more: he was an actual citizen in the here and now of the present life of the heavenly Kingdom, living holocaust of divine energies, witness of God and in a certain sense God himself. As such he was, like the Mother of God herself, a mediator between earth and heaven. He too was a source of mercy, miracle, and guidance, the father of the people among whom he dwelt, their healer and deliverer. Mortal life was a ceaseless warfare between a myriad unseen forces, divine and demoniac, ever-present, overwhelming, unappeasable. Hemmed in by the demons, tempted and overcome, dragged into misfortune or sickness, where else could a man turn but to those who through divine power could subject even the demons to their bidding? Let disease or other affliction come, the holy man was at hand with his healing grace. Let tax-gatherer extort or landlord oppress, the ascetic saint was there to defend against the rapine and the injustice of the powerful. Let the Emperor himself out of considerations of state seek to impose some dogma contrary to holy tradition and, weather-wracked and gaunt, the man of God will descend from pillar or mountain retreat to head the opposition that brings the erring sovereign to heel. For what has the ascetic to fear at the hands of the powerful, even if they are the hands of the Emperor himself? He has already renounced the world and all its ways. All that can be taken from him now is his mortal life, and if he were to lose that through violence laid upon him it might well be but to gain a martyr's crown and so to become an even stronger centre of popular worship and superhuman aid than he already was.

Examples of the exercise of the Saint's influence and authority where Constantinople is concerned are many, but typical of the role that he might play in the city's life is that of St. Daniel the Stylite (d. A.D. 493). Coming originally from Mesopotamia, he entered a monastery at the early age of twelve, full of ardour for the ascetic life. Some time later he made a visit to the 'holy and thrice-blessed Simeon, the man on the pillar', in whose footsteps he felt constrained to follow. Returning once more to his monastery, he was elected Abbot by the brethren, and shortly after that he made another visit to St. Simeon, and then proceeded on the road to Palestine, intending to visit the holy places and above all Jerusalem. On the way, however, he fell in with an old man, in appearance like St. Simeon himself. The old man inquired where Daniel was going, and, on being told, said: *I do not advise you to return for 'he that putteth*

St. Simeon Stylites on
his column. Miniature
from the Menologion
of the Emperor Basil II,
painted about 985.
Vatican, gr. 1613,
fol. 3 r.

*his hand to the plough and turneth back is not fit for the kingdom of Heaven'. But if you will listen to me, there
is one thing I advise.... Verily, verily, verily, behold three times I adjure you by the Lord, do not go to these
places, but go to Byzantium and you will see a second Jerusalem, namely Constantinople; there you can enjoy the
martyrs' shrines and the great houses of prayer, and if you wish to be an anchorite in some desert spot, either in
Thrace or in Pontus, the Lord will not desert you.*

Accordingly, Daniel made his way to Constantinople, where he first established himself in a deserted
and demon-haunted church on the banks of the Bosphorus, and where later, near this same spot, he
took up his stand on the top of a pillar. Meanwhile his fame had spread, and high and low, Emperor and
pauper alike, flocked to him to receive blessing, counsel, or cure. But the chief manifestation of his
public activity, and that which most demonstrates the extraordinary position occupied by the holy man
in the city's life, came when, after a revolt against the Emperor Zeno, Basiliscus, brother of the Empress
Verina, wife of Leo I, and a man of pronounced monophysite leanings, became Emperor. The Life of
the saint gives an account of the event which followed:

*Next Basiliscus—name of ill omen—made an attack upon the churches of God, for he wished to bring them to
deny the incarnate dispensation of God. For this reason he came into conflict with the blessed Archbishop Acacius
(Patriarch of Constantinople 471–489) and sought to malign him so as to bring about his ruin. Directly news
of this attempt reached the monasteries all the monks with one accord assembled in the most holy Great Church
in order to guard the Archbishop. After some consideration the Archbishop ordered all the churches to be draped as
a sign of mourning, and going up into the pulpit he addressed the crowds and explained the blasphemous attempt
which was being made. 'Brethren and children,' he said, 'the time of martyrdom is at hand; let us therefore fight*

95

for our faith and for the Holy Church, our mother, and let us not betray our priesthood.' A great shout arose and all were overcome by tears, and since the Emperor remained hostile and refused to give them any answer, the Archbishop and the archimandrites determined to send to the holy man, Daniel, and give him an account of these things, and this they did.

And it happened by God's providence that on the following day Basiliscus sailed to Anaplus (site of Daniel's hermitage), and sent a chamberlain named Daniel to the holy man to say, 'Do those things which the Archbishop Acacius is practising against me seem just to your angelic nature? for he has roused the city against me and alienated the army and rains insults on me! I beg you, pray for us that he may not prevail against us.' After listening to him the holy man said to Daniel, 'Go and tell him who sent you, "You are not worthy of a blessing for you have adopted Jewish ideas and are setting at nought the incarnation of our Lord Jesus Christ and upsetting the Holy Church and despising His priests. For it is written 'Give not that which is holy unto the dogs, neither cast your pearls before swine'. Know therefore and see, for the God Who rendeth swiftly will surely rend your tyrannous royalty out of your hands."' When the chamberlain heard this answer he said he dared not himself say these things to the Emperor and besought Daniel to send the message in writing, if he would, and seal it with his seal. The holy man yielded to the eunuch's entreaties, wrote a note and after sealing it, gave it to Daniel and dismissed him; and he returned and delivered the sealed note to the Emperor. He opened it and when he learnt the purport of the message he was very angry and immediately sailed back to the city. These things were not hidden from the Archbishop Acacius and his most faithful people; therefore on the following day almost the whole city was gathered together in the Great Church and they kept shouting, 'The holy man for the Church! let the new Daniel save Susanna in her peril! another Elijah shall put Jezebel and Ahab to shame! in you we have the priest of Orthodoxy; he that standeth for Christ will protect His bride, the Church.' And other such exclamations they poured forth with tears.

On the morrow the Archbishop Acacius sent to Daniel some of the archimandrites who were best beloved of God... saying, 'For my sake and the faith's go to the holy man Daniel, throw yourselves before his column and importune him with entreaties saying, "Do you imitate your teacher Christ Who 'bowed the heavens and came down' and was incarnate of a holy virgin and consorted with sinners and shed His own blood to purchase His bride, the Church. Now that she is insulted by the impious, and her people are scattered by fierce wolves and the shepherd tempest-tost, do not ignore my grey hairs but incline your ear and come and purchase your mother, the Church.' And they went and did as they were bid and threw themselves down before the column; and the holy man seeing them lying on the ground was disturbed and began to call to them from above, 'What are you doing, holy fathers, mocking my unworthiness? What is it that you bid me do?' Then they stood up and said, 'That you with God's help should save the faith which is being persecuted, save a storm-tossed church and a scattered flock, and save our priest who, despite his grey hairs, is threatened with death.' And Daniel said to them, 'He is truthful that said, "The gates of hell shall not prevail against the holy Church"; wait patiently therefore where you are and the will of God shall be done; pray then that God may reveal to us what we should do.' And it came to pass that as Daniel was praying in the middle of the night, and as the day dawned—it was a Wednesday—he heard a voice saying distinctly to him, 'Go down with the fathers and do not hesitate; and afterwards fulfil your course in peace!' Obedient therefore to the counsel of the Lord he woke his servants. And they placed the ladder and went up and took away the iron bars round him. And Daniel came down with difficulty owing to the pain he suffered in his feet, and in that same hour of the night he took the pious archimandrites with him and they sailed to the City and entered the church before the day had begun.

And thus it was that when the people came to God's house while, according to custom, the fiftieth psalm was being sung, they saw the holy man in the sanctuary with the Bishop and marvelled; and the report ran through the City that he had come. All the City, and even secluded maidens, left what they had in hand and ran to the Holy Church to see the man of God. And the crowds started shouting in honour of the Saint saying, 'To you we look to banish the grief of the Church; in you we have a high priest; accomplish that for which you came; the crown of your labours is already yours.' But the holy man beckoned with his hand to the people to be silent and addressed them through the deacon, Theoctistus, ' The stretching forth of the hands of Moses, God's servant, utterly destroyed all those who rose up against the Lord's people, both kings and nations; some he drowned in the depths of the sea, others he slew on dry land with the sword and exalted his people; so today, too, your faith which is perfect towards God has not feared the uprising of your enemies, it does not know defeat nor does it need human help; for it is founded on the firm rock of Christ. Therefore do not grow weary of praying; for even on behalf of the chief of the apostles earnest prayer was offered to God, not as if they thought he was deserted by God but because God wishes the flock to offer intercessions for its shepherd. Do you, therefore, do likewise, and amongst us, too, the Lord will quickly perform marvellous things to His glory.' After he had said this they took down all the mourning draperies from the sanctuary and the whole church. Daniel also wrote a letter to the Emperor saying, 'Does this angering of God do you any service? is not your life in His hands? What have you to do with the Holy Church to war against its servants, and prove yourself a second Diocletian?' And many other things like these he wrote both by way of counsel and of blame. When the Emperor received the letter and found that Daniel had come down and was in the church he was stung by the prick of fear and sent back word to him, 'All your endeavour has been to enter the City and stir up the citizens against me; now see, I will hand the City, too, over to you.' And he left the palace and sailed to the Hebdomon (a palace on the Sea of Marmara three miles west of the Golden Gate of the city).

When the holy man heard this news, he took the cross-bearers and the faithful people and bidding the monks guard the Church and the Archbishop he went out.... Thereafter as the holy man with the crowd approached the palace of Hebdomon, a Goth leaned out of a window and seeing the holy man carried along, he dissolved with laughter and shouted, ' See here is our new consul!' And as soon as he said this he was hurled down from the height by the power of God and burst asunder. Then sentinels, or the palace guards, prevented those who had seen the fall from entering into the palace, saying they should have an answer given them through a window. But when the people insisted with shouts that the holy man should enter the palace but received no answer, the servant of God said to them, 'Why do you trouble, children? You shall have the reward promised to peacemakers from God; and since it seems good to this braggart to send us away without achieving anything, let us do to him according to the word of the Lord. For He said to His holy disciples and apostles, " Into whatsoever city or village ye shall enter and they do not receive you, shake off the dust of your feet against them as a testimony to them"; let us therefore do that.' And he first of all shook out his leather tunic and incited the whole crowd to do likewise; and a noise as of thunder arose from the shaking of garments. When the guards who were on duty saw this and heard all the marvellous things God had wrought by Daniel most of them left all and followed him.

When the impious Basiliscus heard what the holy man had done in condemnation of him, he sent two guardsmen of the court and a legal secretary of the Emperor with them to overtake Daniel and implore him to return. These men overtook Daniel and implored him in the name of Basiliscus saying, ' The Emperor says " if indeed I sinned as a man, do you as servant of Christ propitiate Him on my behalf and I will seek in everything to serve God and your Holiness"'.' But the holy man said to them, ' Return and say to the Emperor: Your words of guile and deceit will not avail to deceive my unworthiness, for you are doing nothing but " treasuring up for yourself wrath in the day of wrath"; for in you there is no fruit of good works; wherefore God will shortly confirm His wrath upon you that you may know that " the Most High ruleth over the kingdom of men" and will give it to the good man in preference to you.' With these words he bade the Emperor's secretary to spread out his cloak and after shaking the rest of the dust from his own clothing into the cloak he said, ' Go, carry this to the braggart as a testimony against him and against her who is his confederate and against his wife.' Directly after the messengers had returned and given the Emperor the just man's answer, the tower of the palace fell; since even lifeless things may feel the wrath of God to the salvation of many.

When the just man had arrived at the Golden Gate and saw the concourse of people, he besought them to return each to their own home. But they as with one voice cried, 'We intend to live and die with you; for we have nothing with which to repay you worthily; receive the resolve of your suppliants and lead us as you will, for the Holy Church awaits you.' Whilst the people were uttering these cries two young men afflicted with demons were brought to him; and after he had prayed with tears to God, they were immediately cleansed and they followed him glorifying God. . . .

When he entered into the most holy Cathedral he was received in great sincerity and with acclamation by the Archbishop Acacius and the holy archimandrites and all the reverend clergy and the most pious monks and the most faithful people. And all glorified the merciful God for the marvellous things that they had heard and seen which God had done through him. And they led him into the vestry that he might have a short rest from the pressure of the crowd. . . . When all these things had been thus auspiciously accomplished by the grace of the Lord, and when Basiliscus of ill-omened name had heard from his legal secretary of the Saint's condemnation of him and of the sudden fall of the palace tower, it did not seem to him to augur any good. And immediately without a moment's delay he entered a boat and sailed from the Hebdomon to the City; and the next day he sent senators to the very holy Cathedral to beseech the Saint to take the trouble to come as far as the palace. But he would not consent to go but said, 'Let him come himself to the Holy Church and make his recantation before the precious Cross and the holy Gospel which he has insulted; for I am but a sinful man.' The senators went back and gave this message to the Emperor, whereupon in solemn procession he at once went to the Church. The Archbishop met him with the holy Gospel in the sanctuary and was received by the Emperor with dissimulation; then after the customary prayer had been offered Basiliscus went in with the Archbishop to the holy man. And they both fell at his feet before all the people, both Basiliscus and the Archbishop Acacius. And Daniel greeted them and counselled them to seek the way of peace and for the future to refrain from enmity towards each other. 'For if you are at variance', he said, 'you cause confusion in the holy churches and throughout the world you stir up no ordinary unrest.' The Emperor then made a full apology to the holy man and the people cried out saying, 'Oh Lord, protect both father and sons; it is in thy power to grant us concord between them; let us now hear the Emperor's confession of faith! why are the canons of Orthodoxy upset? why are the Orthodox bishops exiled? To the Stadium with Theoctistus, the Master of the Offices! the Emperor is orthodox! burn alive the enemies of Orthodoxy! send the disturbers of the world into exile! a Christian Emperor for the world! let us hear what your faith is, Emperor!'

These and countless other exclamations the people kept shouting, and all the time the Emperor and the Archbishop lay prostrate on the ground at the holy man's feet.[57]

*

So through such submission; through such ascetic renunciation and withdrawal; through such unsleeping vigilance and prayer; through this constant negation, here, at the heart of the earthly city, at the heart of that civilization of which the earthly city was the visible centre, of this city's very self; through this whole effort to purify and transcend was the restless unremitting desire to keep bright the image of the other city, the heavenly Jerusalem, pursued. Relic and holy cult; icon and living saint: these were the instruments something of whose celestial radiance might be received by whoever with fear, faith, and love would move towards them; through them might be stirred and nourished that sense of the sacred, that sense of the presence of a sustaining, transfiguring power by which alone the earthly city might be preserved from the inhuman and vicious compulsions which must otherwise dominate it. And above all and over all the city's temporal pursuit of a reality not of time's reckoning brooded the chaste image of the Mother of God. Still, grave, imperial, she looked down in love and recognition on the people of her city, she who was at home everywhere and the home of everything, even of what, in its excelling majesty, could have no home; who had yet made Constantinople her special care and charge, so that it was her residence, an abode taken up and sanctified by her favour, the object of her unsparing attention. And the people of Constantinople in their turn reciprocated this sympathy of the Mother of God: knew her as they could not know their own mothers or wives, with some deeper loyalty and attachment and dependence: as one of themselves, her features, the silent compassion of her power, repeated over and over again, invoked over and over again, in mosaic, ivory, enamel, wood, word and chant; in every room of house or palace, above each bed, hanging at every neck, at street-corner or market-place, church or barrack, familiar as sun or rain or as the turning of the seasons, familiar from the first touch of childhood to the last flicker of old age, in joy or sorrow, danger or disease, in the very marrow of thought and feeling itself; and as also the Queen of Heaven, crowned paradigm of all beauty, beyond that of any earthly counterpart, royal lady or emblematic artefact, everlastingly interceding for her people from her station on the borders of the two worlds, created and uncreated, before the throne of God, that the wrath might be turned aside, the scourge recalled, her people forgiven; and listening with maternal solicitude to her city's voice raised in gratitude as the enemy —plague or Saracen, torment within or without—yet once more was driven from the walls by its

Inscription on an ivory cross-reliquary of the end of the tenth century from Constantinople, now at Cortona.

invincible, invisible champion, its inviolate defence: 'To you, the champion Leader, do I, your City, dedicate thank-offerings of victory, for you, O Mother of God, have delivered me from all afflictions; but as you have power invincible, free me from every kind of danger, so that I may cry to you: Hail, unbrided Bride.' [58] This was the reality, this the promise: 'the Jerusalem which is above is free, which is the mother of us all'. [59]

Illustrations on the following pages: Sections of the panorama of Constantinople drawn on 21 leaves by Melchior Lorichs of Flensburg in A.D. 1559, in the time of the Sultan Suleiman the Great. It is the oldest 'naturalistic' portrayal of the city. At this period the horizon is already dominated by the great Turkish mosques with their needle-like minarets; yet the general arrangement of the city remains the same as in the Byzantine period, and even in the form of the mosques as buildings with great central domes the influence of the Byzantine pattern of St. Sophia is operative. A number of churches have remained standing, some converted into mosques and some still serving for Christian worship. Melchior Lorichs's panorama is now in the library of the Royal Netherlands University at Leiden.

Page 101: The Cathedral of St. Sophia without the later outbuildings and buttresses, and with only two minarets, in place of the four which now surround it.

Pages 102–3: The city in the neighbourhood of the Mosque of Sultan Bajezid II. To the right of the great mosque, over a small column, is written 'el masarde formenti', by which is meant the old Byzantine bread-market.

Pages 104–5: Top right, the Mosque of Mohammed II, which was built on the site of the Church of the Apostles. Left of it the ancient Church of St. Andrew.

Pages 106–7: The city in the region of the Mosque of Sultan Selim. Left of this the Churches of St. Tadolf, and of Sts. Peter and Sebastian, once that of St. Theodosia.

Pages 108–9: The Phanar quarter with the city wall at the harbour, which was made double during the siege of 1453. On the wall Lorichs' note can be read: 'When Soldan Mahomit shot down the lowest wall in his assault, this one was built in one night.' In the centre, the buildings of the Patriarchate, which at that time was joined with the Church of the Panaghia Pammakaristos. Over this Lorichs has written: 'The palace, house, or lodging of the Patriarch of the Greeks, the Christians, and of Constantinople.'

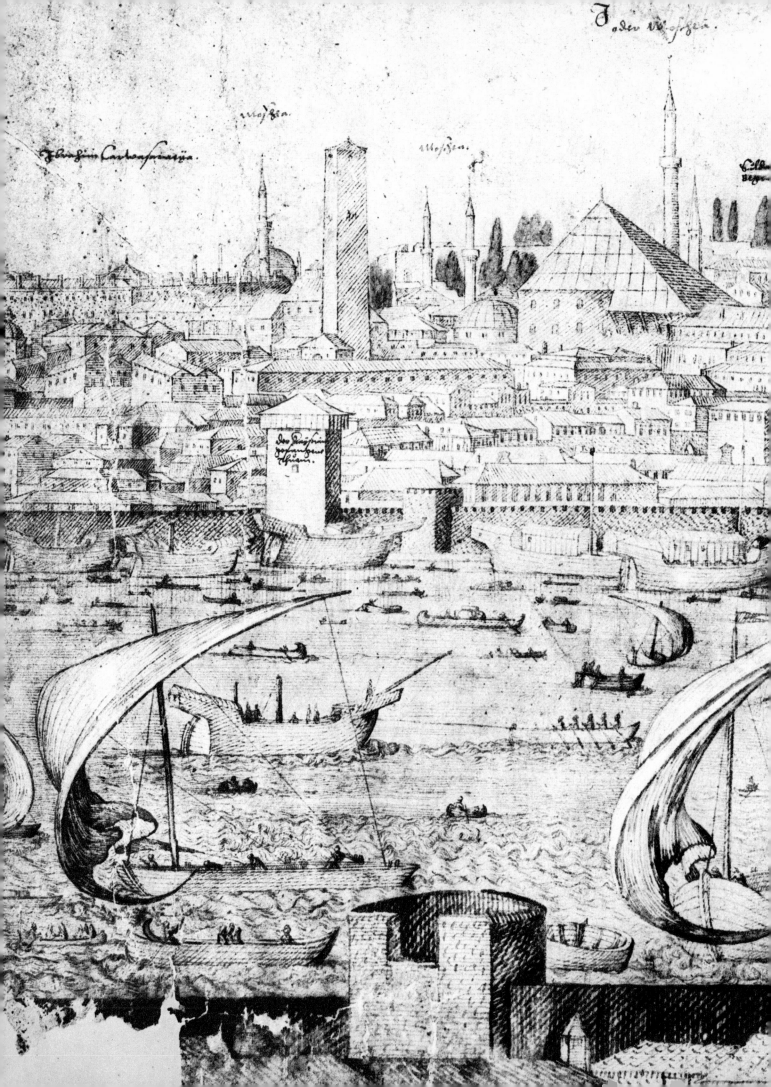

S. Andreas.

The Destruction of an Image

Reflected in the mirror of its own internal iconography, Constantinople presents thus these two images: that of the New Rome, the 'ruling city', through the transfer to it, from the time of its 'consecration' by Sopator, of the whole (pagan and magical) inheritance of the Graeco-Roman world: of the talismans of imperial Rome; of the Tychê and the Palladium; of the bronze eagle attributed by legend to the diabolic art of Apollonius of Tyana and the Calydonian boar whose groin was mutilated by the Empress Euphrosyne in order to secure the success of her divinations; of other statues and emblems erected in public places; also of the works of philosophers and poets, of Greek science, of ways of thought that were 'Sabaean', hermetic, oracular: Irano-Greek horoscopy, the many mantic books, *brontologia, seismologia, lunaria,* the *Oneirokritika* and *Cheiroskopika* of Artemidorus, Gnostic astrology and numerology; of the palatine ritual elaborated round the cult of the Emperor; of the whole structure of imperial government and administration; and that on the other hand of the New Jerusalem, through the transfer to it, from the time of its founding and particularly from the time of the Council of Ephesus (A.D. 432), of Christian relics and above all of relics of the Virgin; through the establishment of its many sanctuaries, again above all of those dedicated to the Virgin, and of its many monasteries where those 'in the habit of angels' maintained the round of ceaseless prayer; through its saints and holy men whose luminous presence was gage of the reality of Christ's promise of his Kingdom. And the question is posed: to what extent did these two images merge in the city's final portrait? (To what extent indeed could they be reconciled?) To what extent did Constantinople, mirror of the whole Byzantine world, witness to the fulfilment of the effort to build the eschatological city of the New Jerusalem upon the imperio-political (and pagan) basis of the New Rome?

For the question which Constantinople ultimately poses is that of the Kingdom of God and its realization. What role in effect has the terrestrial kingdom, the corporate human society or *polis,* in relation to the community of the Christian Church, to God's chosen people? It may be that it has no role at all. It may be that God's activity among mankind is directed solely towards the salvation of individual human souls, and has no manifestation outside this, no manifestation that concerns mankind as a social body. In which case Christ's high-priestly prayer, 'That they all may be one; as thou, Father, art in me, and I in thee, that they also may be one in us' (John 17.21), refers only to the eschatological city 'in heaven' and does not impose upon Christians the task of creating a counterpart on earth, that should serve, in time and space, in history, as a divine instrument through which the living, animate body of humanity is formed in and transformed into the likeness of its eternal paradigm. Or if it does impose upon Christians such a task, then this is fulfilled, not by the will of God operating through the political forms and institutions of the State, but solely by his will operating through the local communities of the Christian Church as an independent society, a *status in statu.* In any case, there is no place, in this view of God's activity among mankind, for the idea that the State may co-operate in the realization of the Kingdom, is, indeed, in some sense the Kingdom itself, the area submissive to the divine revelation of the Gospels and in which the will of God is actualized in the rule of its heirs and custodians.

This view was, we saw, broadly speaking that adopted by Christians in the first centuries after the birth of Christ according to the flesh; and the momentous significance of the Constantinian settlement is that it replaced this view by another, by what in effect is a new idea in history—the idea of the Christian state. According to this view, God's activity among mankind is directed not solely towards the salvation of individual souls but also towards mankind as a whole, towards the working out in time of the corporate salvation of his people. 'My kingdom is not of this world', Christ had said; and although the Byzantines, citizens of the new Christian state that issued from the Constantinian settlement, did not disagree with this, they thought and acted upon what could well be regarded as its corollary, the notion that nevertheless this world could and should participate, by means of an internal transformation begun in and through time, in and through history, in Christ's 'non-worldly' Kingdom. This meant that the social-political organism of humanity, the forms and institutions of the State that moulded its corporate and terrestrial destiny, were no longer a matter of (comparative) indifference to Christians, but came to be regarded as the means whereby mankind must realize itself in the living body of the divine Kingdom, in the Church as the bride of God. What this amounted to in practice was that the whole Graeco-Roman inheritance, that which in fact constituted the forms and institutions of the State, was not to be rejected, but was to be converted, transformed, spiritualized: as Christ had come to fulfil the law and the prophets of the Jews, so the task of the Christian people was now one of fulfilling the law and the prophets of the pre-Christian classical world—the justice and state organization of Rome, the culture of Greece—for these had been not merely human fabrications, but also providential, if partial, preparations for the perfect human society which the Constantinian settlement had inaugurated. There had it is true to be a preliminary battle waged against these very forms and institutions, for they had been regarded as mankind's supreme achievements, ends in themselves, whereas in their new role they were to operate simply as subservient instruments; and such a surrender of status had demanded an initial 'act of violence' against their finalist pretensions.

Thus for good or evil Constantine the Great vitally changed the whole pattern of European history by committing the Empire whose disjointed parts he had, after a series of brilliant victories, knit once more into a coherent unity, to the idea of the Christian state: to the idea that the State could and should be dedicated to the realization of the Kingdom of God; and it is because of this that Constantinople, capital city of this new Christian *imperium* and mirror of its destiny, presents those two images, that of the New Rome and that of the New Jerusalem, in imminent and inescapable confrontation; and the question is posed, we said, of their possible or impossible reconcilability.

What, more closely, is here involved? The instrument of cosmic disunion and strife, that which conceals from us the all-embracing unity and peace of the Kingdom, is the human ego with all the passions and vices that stem from it; and the overcoming of this disintegrating force is by means of an inner transformation that re-establishes the bond connecting human life with its divine principle—a transformation to be achieved, for the Christian, through participation in the inner life of the Church. Rome, after a long and complex historical process, had achieved a formal and external peace and unity —the Pax Romana—in its universal monarchy. This peace and unity of Rome represented the final embodiment of objective reason in the world: by force of reason, expressed in laws and ideas of justice and morality that became the unconditional norms of human life, Rome had imposed on its subject peoples an order in which its ideals of a purely human and rational excellence might be realized. This order it had sought to consolidate in the forms and institutions of the State, with the office of the deified and absolute Caesar at their centre. But this order, and the peace and unity achieved through it, were not only formal and external; they also left untouched, unregenerate, and reprobate that human ego which is the principal instrument of the forces of cosmic disruption and discord. More, it could be said that they were expressions of precisely this ego; for the reason, of which they were the objective embodiment, is itself, when it refuses to recognize what is higher than itself, when it is regarded as an end in itself, precisely the ego's most powerful weapon; and hence its objective realization in the forms and institutions of the State regarded as ends in themselves represents its greatest collective expression. Rome, the terrestrial city as an end in itself, could become the ego's greatest collective expression; and the ritual and symbolic forms in which, as in a mirror, it had sought to eternalize the status of its cosmic and deified king whose continued presence was the guarantee of its absolute rule over the hearts and minds of men, could themselves be inorganic artifices or artificial petrifactions of its non-human malignancy.

What, then, stripped of all ultimate disguise, are in confrontation beneath the imaginary forms of the New Jerusalem and the New Rome are the forces whose realization is in the peace and unity that are 'not of this world' and those that aim, through a system directed towards attaining a purely formal and external state of temporal peace and unity, to perpetuate the reign of that which most prevents our vision of the Kingdom, the human ego. And the task implicit in the acceptance of the idea of a Christian state, a Christian City, was that of transforming the latter by the former, of so piercing the crust of the human ego, and the forms and institutions of the terrestrial city of the New Rome in which it was expressed, with the transfiguring light of the New Jerusalem that they too would reflect something of the divine-human reality of the Incarnate God in whom all are one and the One is all.

Here, though, where Constantinople is concerned, that task was bedevilled from the start by the ambiguity implicit in the very act of the city's founding as a Christian city by Constantine the Great: was Constantinople dedicated as a Christian city for reasons of the Kingdom or for reasons of the State? Did Constantine accept for himself and his successors the role of Christian Emperor for the love and glory of God or because such an acceptance seemed the most likely way of securing the continued integrity of the Empire for which he was responsible? For if Constantinople poses the question of the Kingdom of God, it also poses the question of the Anti-Christ: since the ultimate perversion, that in which the image of the Beast is concealed, is to make use of the forms, the loyalties and symbols of the heavenly City in order to consolidate the triumph of the reign of the 'prince of this world'. What one witnesses then is not the christianizing of the forms of society but the socializing of the forms of Christianity—the petrifaction of the living, divine-human spontaneity of these forms and their reduction to static, inorganic objects of an idolatry that imprisons its victims in a mirror-world in which the human image is denied. So that the whole question of the possible or impossible reconciliation of the two images reflected in the iconography of the Byzantine capital is complicated from the start by the task of determining whether, or to what extent, the idea of the New Jerusalem is made to serve as a means of maintaining the stability of the New Rome, the idea of the Pax Christiana is made to serve the consolidation of the Pax Romana.

To say all this may in fact be to do nothing less than to point to the profoundly paradoxical nature of the idea of the Christian State itself—an idea which must always be a stumbling-block to philosophers and historians because it is paradoxical, because it is based finally upon irreconcilabilities, in the sense that while, by the terms of their Revelation, Christians are bound to seek to realize it, it is, because of the very condition of the world—'fallen', marked by ancestral sin—in which and by which it must be achieved, nevertheless impossible to realize; in the sense that while rooted in Christianity itself, while demanding its fulfilment in time and space, in history, in the social-political organism of humanity, its consummation lies in the surpassing of those temporal and spatial artefacts or forms that limit its existence: for ultimately, for those who are 'beneath the veil', the Kingdom, on which the idea of the Christian City depends and in whose name it is built, is not a State but a Calling, a Desire, for the things that are not to destroy the things that are, for what really is to destroy what only seems to be: *Veni, creator spiritus*. So that ultimately too the role of this City, Rome *or* Babylon, is fulfilled in having made it possible, if only for brief moments, for the prophetic voice of the New Jerusalem to be heard through the cries—of pleasure, vice, restlessness, or despair—of the daily dying life of its citizens; and its supra-historic destiny is achieved, not in the constructions, symbolic or ritual, in which it is imaged here below, not in the artificial or emblematic décor of its social and religious life, but in a reality which transcends its fall.

Liturgical fan, of silver.
Sixth century. Istanbul.

To trace the apocalyptic history of the fall of Constantinople—that history in which the questions posed above might be answered—would be to exceed, among other things, the scope of this book. But any account of it would have to include at least some description of the Byzantines' own attitude to the fate of their city; would have to show how the life of this city was vitiated from within by the growth of superstition (astrologers, necromancers), by natural sickness, by cruelty and greed, by a moral and intellectual decline; and was suffocated from without by the siege and attacks (the wars of Gog and Magog) of barbarians, Goths, Avars, Bulgars, Russians, until it was captured and violated by French, German, and Italian crusaders in 1204, to fall finally, after a crippled existence of a further two hundred and fifty-odd years, the first fifty-seven of which were under a Latin Emperor, to the Turks, to an army of Janissaries sworn to a martyr's death in sacred battle.

Where the attitude of the Byzantines to the fate of their city is concerned,[60] one may recall the words reported to have been used at the time of Constantine's consecration of his capital: 'Then the city that was called Constantinople was saluted with acclamations, when the priest cried aloud: "O Lord, guide it well for infinite ages."' This New Rome, capital of the new Christian State built by Constantine, itself destined to be the last world power, would continue until the Second Coming of Christ (for from the start the city was linked to an eschatological destiny). *Tell me*, his disciple, Epiphanius, questioned his tenth-century Master, St. Andrew the Fool for Christ, *Tell me please how and when the end of this world (will be)? What are the beginnings of the throes? And how will men know that (the end) is close, at the doors? By what signs will the end be indicated? And whither will pass this city, the New Jerusalem? What will happen to the holy temples standing here, to the venerated icons, the relics of the Saints, and the books? Please inform me; for I know what God said about thee and those who are like thee: it is given unto you to know the mysteries of the kingdom of heaven; even more the mysteries of this world.* And St. Andrew began his reply: *Concerning our city know that it will in no way be terrified by any nation till the consummation of time, for no one will ever ensnare it or take it; because it has been given to the Mother of God, and no one will tear it from Her holy arms....*[61] St. Andrew's words have of course a 'non-literal' validity; but they

could also be taken quite literally; and indeed so inseparably linked, or confused, could the idea of the New Jerusalem be with that of the New Rome, that of the Church *(ekklesia)* with that of the earthly kingdom *(basileia)*, that, finally, of the end of Constantinople with that of the end of the world and the Second Coming, that as late as the end of the fourteenth century, when the city had already once been captured and was anyhow still threatened on all sides, the Patriarch Antonius could write to the Grand Prince of Russia, Vasili I, how 'it is not possible for Christians to have a Church and not to have an Empire' and how the Emperor of the Empire must be that of Constantinople, even if, by the permission of God, the nations (i.e. the Turks) now encircle the government and the imperial residence.[62]

However this may have been, and however strong the belief that its end would coincide with the end of the world, the sense of the city's impending and inevitable doom was always present. Unlike the Romans, the Byzantines had few illusions about the ultimate fate of their city. And they were continually preoccupied with this fate. In the masterpieces of ancient art with which the city was crowded, in the figures of gods and heroes, they saw good or evil genii, talismans guaranteeing the security of the city or omens announcing, through mysterious inscriptions or obscure bas-reliefs, its terrifying destruction, the history of its last days. At the Forum of Constantine, on columns standing at the square's centre, on the statues of animals decorating the quarter of the Artopolia, on other columns, were strange signs, hieroglyphic or astronomic, that told, sometimes 'with names', of the city's future and its fate. The Hippodrome was full of prophetic statues, among which of particular significance were the bronze steles where Apollonius of Tyana had inscribed 'the whole story of the last days'. In the Forum of Constantine also this same magician had set down the names of all the Emperors that were to rule over the city and the Empire. In the Forum of Taurus was an equestrian statue that had been brought from Antioch; according to some, the rider was Bellerophon, according to others, Joshua the son of Nun; and again the bas-reliefs carved round its pedestal told of the last days, the end of the city, 'when the Russians would take Constantinople'. But although all agreed that in these inscriptions and reliefs, in the hieroglyphics and signs, were concealed accounts of the city's final doom, no one could interpret them. Or at least no one could interpret them until after the event to which they referred had taken place. Robert of Clari speaks of this when he describes the prophetic columns he saw after the Latin conquest of the city:

There was elsewhere in the city still another great marvel. There were two columns, each of them at least three times the reach of man's arms in thickness and at least fifty toises in height. And hermits used to live on the tops of these columns in little shelters that were there, and there were doors in the columns by which one could ascend. On the outside of these columns there were pictured and written by prophecy all the events and all the conquests which have happened in Constantinople or which were going to happen. But no one could understand the event until it had happened, and when it had happened the people would go there and ponder over it, and then for the first time they would see and understand the event. And even this conquest of the French was written and pictured there and the ships in which they made the assault when the city was taken, and the Greeks were not able to understand it before it had happened, but when it had happened they went to look at these columns and ponder over it, and they found that the letters which were written on the pictured ships said that a people, short haired and with iron swords, would come from the West to conquer Constantinople![63]

And elsewhere, too, it is recorded that there were sculptures believed to represent the prophecies of the Sibyl, and that these included ships with ladders and men on the ladders intending to assault the city; and that when the people of Constantinople saw ladders erected on the Venetian ships by the crusaders, they recognized the warning of the sculptures, and mutilated them with stones and hammers, so that they might bring bad luck upon the invaders.

Illustration opposite: The Blessed Virgin Hodigitria, from a mosaic of the beginning of the twelfth century in the south gallery of St. Sophia.

117

This sense of the end, this preoccupation with an inevitable and violent doom, may be seen simply as a reflection of natural fears arising from the experience of so many attacks and sieges—there had been seventeen such unsuccessful attacks and sieges before the Latin conquest of the city; from the knowledge that on all sides enemies, potential or actual, thronged. Or it may be seen as something deeper, as a reflection of a kind of collective guilt, a guilt bred from many fertile, if fetid, sources: from the knowledge of the city's unpurged pagan past, of the long centuries of the worship of false gods that was implicit in the very fact of its foundation, intertwined with the very roots of its existence; from the knowledge that these same gods, these powers and principalities of the outer darkness, were too strong, too firmly entrenched within the city walls, ever to be exorcised by anything less than the city's annihilation, and that, even if they had been deprived of official worship, of official status, they still lurked, profligate and unrepentent, beneath the formal surface of the city's public and private life, ready to break through with a crudity and a rapacity unknown in the time of their ancient recognition; from the knowledge that this chosen people of the New Jerusalem, the elect of God, had themselves fallen away from the high calling to which they had been summoned, that they were riddled with the most abject superstition, had turned their sacred relics into objects of idolatry, guarantees of temporal welfare, insurance policies for material rewards; that they were lulled into sloth by a sense of superiority based no longer on any natural or spiritual pre-eminence but simply on an excess of privilege and on an uncontrollable vanity; from the knowledge too that behind the city's splendid décor lay the ferment of the impure, violent deeds which this décor had witnessed; that the meticulous details of court etiquette, the trappings, the gilt, the lofty images, concealed an appalling horror; that the nameless enigmatic priests of this hieratic imperial society, stiff in their brocades, rigid as effigies, compelled to act out, year by year, a ritual of an intricacy that defeats analysis, yet bled or suffocated beneath the copes and mitres of decorum, caught in the eternal recurrence of a mirror-world of atrophied inorganic symbols from which they could never hope to escape; and that on the other side of this mirror-world (that 'other side' of which works like Procopius' *Secret History* permit glimpses), beneath the formal perfection of the whole 'artifice of eternity' which the city represented, smouldered the unredeemed powers of hysteria, destructiveness, and corruption.

Constantinople, from Hartmann Schedel's Chronicle of 1493.

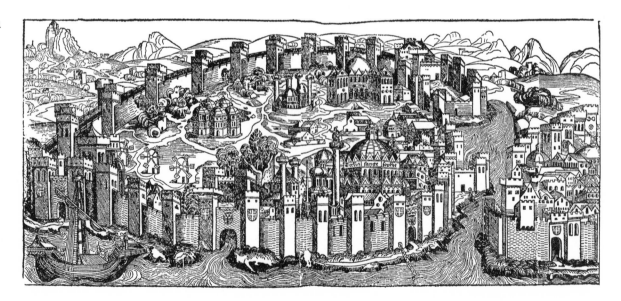

Be this as it may, it is certainly true that every assault, internal or external, plague, earthquake, war, was felt to be a divine visitation, a punishment for sins committed. The theme is constant, almost monotonously so, throughout the whole period of the city's historical existence: 'What is this? What is this grievous and heavy blow and wrath?' asked the Patriarch Photius, on the occasion of the Russian attack on Constantinople in 860; and he continues: *Is it not for our sins that all these things have come upon us? Are they not a condemnation and a public parading of our transgressions? Does not the terror of things present indicate the awful and inexorable judgement of the future? ... Verily, sins diminish tribes, and sin is like a two-edged sword for those who indulge in it. We were delivered from evils which often had held us; we should have been thankful, but we showed no gratitude. We were saved, and remained heedless; we were protected and were contemptuous. For these things punishment was to be feared. O cruel and heedless minds, worthy to suffer every misfortune and distress! From those who owed us small and trifling things we made relentless exaction; we chastised them. We forgot to be grateful when the benefit had gone by .... We enjoyed ourselves, and grieved others; we were glorified, and dishonoured others; we grew strong and throve, while waxing insolent and foolish. We became fat, gross and thick..., and like a maddened heifer we raged against the Lord's commandments, and we disdained his ordinances. For this reason there is a sound of war and great destruction in our land. For this reason the Lord hath opened his treasury and brought forth the weapons of his anger. For this reason a people has crept down from the north, as if it were attacking another Jerusalem, and nations have been stirred up from the end of the earth, holding bow and spear.... Come unto me, O most compassionate of prophets, bewail Jerusalem with me—not the ancient one, the metropolis of one nation, which grew up from a root with twelve offshoots, but the metropolis of the entire universe, as much of it as is adorned by the Christian creed, which lords it in antiquity, in beauty, in size, splendour, in the multitude and magnificence of its inhabitants. Bewail with me this Jerusalem, not yet captured and fallen down, but standing nigh to be captured, and rocked by the calamities we behold. Bewail with me the queen of cities, not as she is led away captive, but whose hopes of salvation are in captivity. Seek water for the head and fountains of tears for the eyes, pity her and mourn for her, since she weeps sore in the night, and the tears are on her cheeks, and there is none to comfort her; since Jerusalem has sinned a sin; therefore has she come into tribulation....* [64]

Another contemporary criticism, by Joseph Bryennios, is more impressive, not simply because it repeats the same theme in more detail, but because, being written in the fourteenth century, when the evil, internal and external, had gathered head, had broken through the mirror, and when it was now clear that the centre could no longer hold, it shows that the Byzantines—or at least some of them—could still measure up to the state of their corruption. They could still see their misfortunes as the consequence not merely of natural or 'historical' processes (the inevitable organic 'decline of states', the superior military organization of the Turks, and so on), but also of a metaphysical justice. Thus they could still attach their history to its principle, could still live and possess what one may call a sacred history (a history, that is, in which the sense of a supra-historic destiny reveals the significance of temporal occurrences), and were not simply blind victims of a series of meaningless and mechanical events. The following extract, dealing with the intellectual and moral state of the citizens of Constantinople and of the causes of their plight, is taken from Bryennios' criticism:

If the sight of the punishments that God inflicts on us provokes astonishment and perplexity, let our extravagances be considered and it will be found surprising that we are not struck by the thunderbolt. There is not a single form of perversity that we are not skilled in practising all our life. And these are the proofs of this: we are baptized, some by a single, others by a triple, immersion, and the name of the Holy Trinity is invoked either once or thrice. Most of us are not only ignorant of what being a Christian means, but even of how to make the sign of the cross; or, if we know how, we are ashamed to make it. Our priests are ordained for money and, like most people, have relations with their wives before marriage. Remission of sins and communion of the divine gifts are accorded in exchange for presents. Monks, quite shamelessly, and in spite of their vows of chastity, cohabit with nuns. We fail to avenge the name of God when it is blasphemed, when we should die for Him. We bestow the common name of the enemies of the cross on one another, and have it continually on our lips. Daily we anathematize and pour curses on ourselves and others. Without hesitating we take speakable or unspeakable oaths and at all times we swear falsely by the redoubtable and holy name of our God and Saviour, and this without any need. We complain to God whether it rains or fails to rain. that it is hot, that it is cold, that He gives riches to one and leaves the other poor, that a south wind rises, that a gale blows from the north; and quite simply we set ourselves up as intransigent judges of God. Many of us impudently blaspheme against the Orthodox Faith, the Cross, the Law, the Saints, God Himself, while even an infidel would not do as much.... We impart disorderly movement to the holy icons and pretend to read the future from these movements. Most of our sins are unconfessed, so unpardonable are they. Interrogating all parts of our bodies we put them at the service of the enemy: do we not conjecture the future by the itching of the hands or of the nose, the twitching of an eyelid, the buzzing of the ear, in short by all the natural manifestations of our organs? We see auguries in the replies and salutations of men. We note the cries of domestic birds, the flight and call of crows and we draw omens from them. We deceive ourselves with the belief of astrologers that our existence is directed by the Hours, by Lot, the Fates, Destiny, the signs of the Zodiac and the Planets. We are certain that Nereids live in the sea and that Genii rule over each spot.... Some of us worship and greet the new moon. We celebrate the kalends, we wear the rings of Mars, we decorate our dwelling-places with May-wreaths.... We take note of dreams and believe that they tell us the future. We hang amulets at our necks and practise divination. We resort daily to magicians, to diviners, to gipsies, to sorcerers; for every sickness we seek a cure in magic and by it we cast spells on men and beasts. Through incantations we seek to promote the fertility of our fields, the growth and health of our herds, success in hunting, an abundant grape-harvest. We flee ever further from virtue and search out vice increasingly. Friendship is banished and malice has taken its place. Brother exploits brother, and each friend follows the path of treachery. There is no mercy, no compassion, only hatred and impudence. Our masters are iniquitous; those who govern our affairs, rapacious; our judges, corrupt; our arbitrators, liars; citizens, deceivers; countrymen, without judgement; and all in general are abject. Our virgins are more outrageous than prostitutes; widows are curious beyond reason; married women scorn a faith they do not keep; the young are lost in debauchery; the old given over to drink. Women married to priests insult their status; priests have forgotten God; monks have completely strayed from the right path; people in the world are so lost that with words they give themselves the external appearance of piety, while inwardly they deny all virtue. Our face is that of a prostitute and a sinner. Such is our hardness of heart, our forgetfulness, our blindness, that we no longer believe we commit deeds of wickedness or suffer from them, when in reality we are their authors and their victims.... It is these sins and others like them that make us worthy of the punishments with which God visits us in payment for these faults and other depravities equally grave. It is thus that God punishes His people.[65]

*

Strong as may have been the feeling that the multitude of the city's sins made divine vengeance inevitable, there is no doubt that it was given support by the frequency with which this vengeance seemed about to strike the city in the form of attacks from foreign enemies. The city was a city under siege, actual or potential—under siege for its life: involved incessantly in the wars of Gog and Magog, Barbarians, Avars, Bulgars, Russians, Turks—as remarked, seventeen times already before the Latin conquest of 1204 they had pitted themselves unsuccessfully against the city's massive walls. The memory of one assault had hardly time to fade before the spectre of another rose on the horizon. And from the time of the Turkish occupation of Asia Minor in the latter half of the eleventh century the threat, of attack, of spoliation, was constantly present, was almost indeed visible. Yet it was not in fact from that quarter that the first crippling blow fell, even if it was from there that came the final defeat. For, ironically,

Saracen assault on Constantinople. Miniature from the MS. of Skilitzes in the National Library, Madrid.

it was to their 'schismatic' Christian brothers of the West that the Byzantines first surrendered their city.

Not that the Byzantines always regarded the peoples of Western Europe as their brothers. Only too often when they referred to them, it was simply to class them as 'barbarians', as those beyond the pale, lesser breeds without the law. Indeed, by the twelfth century (the period here in question), many could look upon the whole of the West as one gigantic apostasy from Christ and genuine culture. So 'greedy for gain' were the Western races, wrote the imperial princess and chronicler, Anna Comnena, that they would 'sell for an obol even what they hold most dear', including their wives and children. 'Such is the race of Celts', she elsewhere apostrophizes, 'changeable and in a swift turning-point of time carried in opposite directions, and you may see the same man sometimes boasting that he will upset the whole earth, sometimes cringing and brought down to the very dust, especially when he falls in with stronger minds.' [66] Insolent, primitive, uncultured, bellicose, predatory, verbose (their endless loquacity kept the Emperor Alexius I standing for so long that it was indirectly one of the main causes of his gout), entirely lacking in the intelligence or refinement of the Byzantines or Moslems: so might they be characterized by imperial scribes. Yet even so, for one very important reason they were of considerable concern: their warlike virtues could be employed in relieving the Turkish pressure on Constantinople's Asiatic flank. It was this which led the Byzantine Emperors of these final centuries to seek to encourage in the West, by overtures to the Pope, matrimonial alliances, even apostasy to the Roman faith, what was ultimately to be so fatal for their capital city: a crusade against the infidel, not because they had particular interest in delivering the Holy Places, but because they thought they might be able to use it incidentally for reconquering such of their lost Asia Minor cities as Nicaea or Antioch.

On their side the peoples of the West had many reasons for an interest in Constantinople. First of all, the Papacy, in the name of that same Christian State which underlay the imperial idea of Byzantium, and thus by embarking on a policy in which the confusion of spiritual and temporal posed the same questions as those posed by the Christian State of Byzantium—the Papacy had set out upon the task of uniting Europe under its own leadership; and it was not to be long before papal canonists were formulating the theory that the Pope, as head of the Holy Roman Empire, was the unique legitimate heir of the Roman Caesar, and thus was obliged to accept the temporal role and responsibilities that went with this office. This meant among other things that he had to fight the Empire's wars. Fortunately, or unfortunately, he was able to combine the duty of fighting these wars with that of uniting Europe under his leadership. For centuries an increasing stream of pilgrims from the West had been visiting the Holy Land, and this traffic had not come to a halt even when, in 1009, the Shiite Hakin had destroyed the Holy Sepulchre. But when the Seljuk Turks took Jerusalem in 1070, and a year later defeated the Byzantine armies at Manzikert, thus occupying a large part of the imperial territories of Asia Minor, the pilgrimages were stopped. At least, they were stopped in practice. But the theory of the pilgrimage to the Holy Places, of the importance of a physical journey to the actual scenes of Christ's historical life and more particularly of his Passion, of the whole drama of Golgotha, grew in intensity—grew as part of that cult of the literal physical identification of the Christian with the sufferings of Christ of which another aspect was the desire to receive Christ's physical wounds, the stigmata, in the human body. The consequence of this was a growing demand for a war to liberate the Holy Places from the hand of the infidel that now possessed them. And this demand could be exploited, in poetry, pontifical epistles, sermons of pro- paganda, to promote the idea of a sacred war, of a pan-European crusade, in which the nobility of Western Europe should join forces and sink their differences in the pursuit, under the direction of the Papacy, of a common aim, the conquest of the Holy Land, the liberation of the Temple, of the terrestrial setting of the Nativity, of the miracles of the Gospels, of the mystery of the Redemption. In this way the idea of a crusade might serve as a unifying force operating in favour of the realization of that Christian state of which the Papacy was to assume the spiritual and temporal control: it promised the satisfaction of the religious aspirations of the people, in that it was an *artifice de Dieu* that opened the way to the Heavenly Jerusalem (since the ninth century the Roman Church had promised the absolution of sins and the palm of martyrdom to whoever was killed defending the faith); of the terrestrial aspirations of the nobility, or robber-barons, of the Norman kingdoms and of Northern France, in that it would give access to new territorial areas from which large estates might be carved out; and of the 'imperial' aspirations of the Papacy, in that it could unite Europe in a common cause under papal leadership.

None of this of course need have involved Constantinople at all. The idea of a crusade had for the Byzantines little of the significance which it possessed for the Latins. To start with, Constantinople was its own 'holy land', had its own 'holy places', was the New Jerusalem. What, the Byzantine might have asked, has Golgotha that Constantinople does not have? But this was precisely one of the reasons why Western attention turned upon it: it was itself a pilgrim centre for the Westerners, one of the *loca sancta* of the Christian world, precisely because it held so many of the major Christian relics, and parti- cularly the relic of the Cross; precisely because it was a New Jerusalem. And now, from the Western 'papal' point of view, it possessed these 'holy places' of its relics illicitly, just as the Turks possessed the holy places of Jerusalem illicitly. It had forfeited the right to give them sanctuary: forfeited it by breaking with the Church at Rome, through failing to recognize the papal claim to supremacy. 'Great pain and universal sorrow obsess me', wrote Pope Gregory VII to Hugh, Abbot of Cluny, in, or soon after, 1074. 'The Church of the Orient is moving further from the Catholic faith, and the devil, having killed it spiritually, causes its members to perish in the flesh by the sword of his henchmen lest at any time divine grace bring them to a better mind.' It is thus that the principles of the sacred war could be invoked where Constantinople was concerned just as they could be where the Holy Land was concerned: in both cases it was a question of liberating the sacred things of Christianity from the hands of those who now unlawfully possessed them; and although the Pope did not directly invoke them to promote such a crusade against the city, yet, according to Villehardouin, the Roman clergy outside Constantinople in 1204 used the same arguments and promised the same indulgences to the besieging crusading forces of the West as were used and promised by the Papacy when the object of attack was the armies of Islam: *C'est pourquoi nous vous disons, fait le clergé, que la bataille est droite et juste. Et si vous avez droite intention de conquérir la terre et de la mettre en l'obédience de Rome, tous ceux de vous qui y mourront confessés auront le pardon que le pape vous a octroyé. Sachez que cette chose fut un grand encouragement pour les barons et pour les pèlerins.*[67] And it must be remembered also in this connexion that Constantinople was the city of the Virgin, and that the cult of the Virgin had been growing steadily in the West during this period; hence the arguments for delivering the sacred things of Christianity from the 'godless' city derived additional appeal from the knowledge that in this city lay such precious relics of the Virgin as her girdle and her robe. (The connexion between Chartres, the cult of the Virgin, and the crusades is for example intimate.)

If a 'crusade' against Constantinople promised thus to satisfy the religious aspirations of the crusaders in much the same way as a crusade to the Holy Land, it promised to satisfy their rapacity to an even greater extent. The Normans and Germans had already had their appetites whetted for what was known to be 'the richest city of the world'. From the tenth century onwards the East-West cultural flow, in the form of miniatures, gold-work, and enamel-work, and of influence on murals and architecture, had continually increased, and this evidence of more or less unlimited treasure and refinement was added to, particularly in Eastern Europe, by Byzantium's own political and cultural propaganda through expensive and rare gifts, crowns or imperial ladies, as 'honoraria': the lower loop of the existing sacred crown of Hungary, St. Stephen's crown, for example, is in fact the famous Ducas crown presented to the wife of King Geza I, a niece of the Emperor Nicephorus III Botaneiates (1078–1081). So great was Byzantium's prestige in Western eyes, so much was Constantinople the universal paradigm, that it provided the model for all other emperors, kings, and princes, for court life and crown, politics and pageantry, and this even while those whose imitation was most marked were plotting against the city: Henry VI, for instance (1190–1197), Barbarossa's son, and from 1184 heir apparent of the Normans in Sicily, laid plans for the systematic conquest of Constantinople. Finally, where the Papacy's 'imperial' aspirations were concerned, a 'crusade' against Constantinople promised to satisfy these as much or even more than a crusade to the Holy Land, for not only could it result in the subjection of Byzantium's imperial territories to Roman rule, but also it was only through Constantinople that papal domination of Eastern Europe, Russia, and the Near East could be brought about.

It was the combination of all this (and to it must be added the commercial enterprise of Venice and Genoa, as well as their commercial rivalry) that accounts for the growing covetous interest of the West in Constantinople and for the linking of this interest with the idea of a crusade: through such a variety and coincidence of impressive motives the psychological ground was prepared for what has been called an event unparalleled in history, the diversion of the Fourth Crusade (it had been dispatched to Egypt) and the sack of Constantinople by the crusaders in 1204. This is not the place to retrace the sordid steps that led to this diversion, or to give details of the sack itself. But the words of the historian may again be quoted: *For nine centuries the great city had been the capital of Christian civilization. It was filled with works of art that had survived from ancient Greece and with the masterpieces of its own exquisite craftsmen. The Venetians indeed knew the value of such things. Wherever they could they seized treasures and carried them off to adorn the squares and churches and palaces of their town. But the Frenchmen and Flemings were filled with the lust for destruction. They rushed in a howling mob down the streets and through the houses, snatching up everything that glittered and destroying whatever they could not carry, pausing only to murder or to rape, or to break open the wine-cellars for their refreshment. Neither monasteries nor churches nor libraries were spared. In St. Sophia itself drunken soldiers could be seen tearing down the silken hangings and pulling the great silver iconostasis to pieces, while sacred books and icons were trampled under foot. While they drank merrily from the altar-vessels a prostitute sat herself on the Patriarch's throne and began to sing a ribald French song. Nuns were ravished in their convents. Palaces and hovels alike were entered and wrecked. Wounded women and children lay dying in the streets. For three days the ghastly scenes of pillage and bloodshed continued, till the huge and beautiful city was a shambles.... No one, wrote Villehardouin, could possibly count the gold and silver, the plate and the jewels, the samite and silks and garments of fur, vair, silver-grey and ermine; and he added, on his own learned authority, that never since the world was created had so much been in a city.* [68]

*

Standing at the centre of a vast network not only of European and Asiatic trade-routes but also of European and Asiatic consciousnesses, Constantinople owed its existence quite as much to the image of itself which it cast or begot in the mirror of surrounding minds as to the facets of these minds which it reflected in its own internal iconography: was in fact a product of precisely this two-way traffic or confrontation; and the corollary of this is that its historical destiny was determined and revealed through this same traffic or confrontation. We have sought to trace, however sketchily, the form and fate that emerge from the compound of the centre and the West; it remains, to complete the triptych, the city's final portrait, to say something of the Eastern image.

The confrontation between Constantinople and the Islamic world, that world of which, in this context, Baghdad was the centre, was as that of a mirage reflected in a mirror, a mirage of gold in a mirror of silver, a mirage of beauty in an iconoclastic mirror. [69] For the image of Constantinople that was strongest in the Islamic mind was that of a golden coin, an image that was both sacred and royal and whose minting was reserved exclusively to the *basileus*. The immense wealth of Constantinople, retained more or less intact until its sack by the crusaders, and symbolized by the magnificent bezant, was both a challenge and an affront to Islam, whose own wealth, that of the Baghdad mints, derived first of all from the Sassanid stocks of silver captured at Ctesiphon in 639 (in traditional symbolism, it will be remembered, gold is the royal irradiation, masculine, while silver is feminine). And although Islam minted a gold coinage in 696, thus violating the sacred privilege which the Byzantine Emperor retained until 1204, it remained this reflecting feminine moon stirred by and drawn to, in need and envy, the provocative masculine splendour of Byzantium's gold-emblazoned sun.

In the second place, Constantinople was the image of a virginal beauty, a virginal icon, mosaic, or painting on a golden ground. The role which the presence of its numerous icons played in rousing the iconoclastic religious conscience of Islam against Constantinople, as centre of the Christian world, is hard to estimate, though from this point of view the policy of the icon-destroying Byzantine Emperors may be seen as a self-defensive gesture in the face of threatened Moslem attacks on their capital city (the first of these attacks, in 674–677, had already taken place some fifty years before the iconoclast Emperors began their destruction of the icons). But the religious impulsion of the Islamic warrior towards Constantinople was not primarily in order to destroy its religious images (there was, especially until the expulsion of the Orthodox communities from Asia Minor in 1922, ample evidence for the respect with which Islam could regard Christian icons in the fact that many icon-adorned sanctuaries—Seidnaya is an example—were shared between Christians and Moslems), nor to lay violent hands on its tantalizing

physical beauty. It had much more in common with the religious motive of the crusader: that by means of the sacred war (the *djihâd*) the faithful could cast off the burdens of terrestrial existence, could do penance for the sinfulness of life in a corrupt world, could, through his death in battle, his martyrdom, achieve the eternal beauty of Paradise. Constantinople was an image of this paradisiacal beauty, a radiant reliquary, the veil of the all-pure Virgin, Panakhrantos: an image which had been obscured and corrupted by the demoniac atmosphere distilled from the city's thousand pagan talismans, by its crass superstition, by its moral obliquity, by the perversity, finally, of the Christian Trinitarian faith that seemed to violate, to introduce a relativity into, the Absolute Unity of God on which the Moslem insisted. And if his ascetic monotheism impelled the Moslem towards Constantinople, this was not so much to destroy as to affirm and to liberate: to affirm the superiority of the Absolute Unity over the Trinity, of the Transcendence over the Incarnation; and to liberate the city from captivity, to lift the stained Byzantine veil from the true beauty of the divine mystery (one thinks of the symbolic value of the woman's veil in Islam), and to restore the true Christian image, that contained in the two pure Names of Jesus and Mary, to its original purity. To this must be added the impulsion of less ascetic appetites: appetites stirred by the sight, at Baghdad, of the physical beauty of Greek slaves of both sexes, young men and girls who seemed to be the living images of those *huris* and *ghilmān* reserved for the delectation of Moslems in Paradise or, by reduction to this level, of the Moslem soldiers who would pierce the wall of Constantinople; and these appetites also found their release in the frightful violation of the city in the nights and days following the dawn of 29 May, a Tuesday, 1453.

Finally, and above all, Constantinople was linked with the eschatological fulfilment of Islam, the promised fulfilment of the ordeal *(Mubāhala)* proposed in vain at Medina by the Prophet to the 'maternal uncles' of the first Abbassid. And here the eschatological hope of Christian Constantinople came face to face with its opposite, that of Islam: the one looking towards a glorious *beyond*, towards the transfiguration, the reign of Christ and the coming of his Kingdom, Heavenly Jerusalem, and thus to be accomplished through the destruction of the terrestrial city ('for here we have no continuing city, but we seek one to come': Hebrews 13.14), the other towards a supreme Battle fought out here below, when Jesus, whose first coming had been humble, pacific, and hidden, would appear now as the Warrior Leader of the faithful to establish on earth the Reign of Justice. Not only do these two awaited eschatological destinies here confront one another; they also, even in their opposition, coincide, become the gage of each other's truth. For in the Islamic *hadiths*, according to certain Turkish interpretations, the taking of Constantinople was associated with the coming of Dadjdjal ('Anti-Christ') and the final 'hour': 'Blessed the army that will take it (Constantinople)', for it will be commanded by the awaited Chief, Muntazir, who with the army that has conquered the New Rome will later, when Jesus descends from Heaven, go to Jerusalem to kill the Anti-Christ. It is thus that the city, prefiguration of Paradise, became for the Islamic Turks the object of sacred spiritual war, to be taken not simply at the point of lances but also by the arrows of prayer and the battering-rams of an ascetic discipline.

So it was that on Friday, 23 March 1453, the young Sultan Mohammed II set out from Adrianople for Constantinople with 12,000 Janissaries, those 'New Troops' formed, in 1326, to constitute an élite religious-military fraternity under an ascetic misogamist rule which derived from that of the dervish saint, Hadji Bektash, and whose members were recruited, with an ingenuity that might be admirable did it appear less diabolic, not from the Turks but from the finest-formed male children of the Sultan's Christian subjects. Diplomatic negotiations between Emperor and Sultan were at an end. *As it is clear,* wrote the Emperor, Constantine XI Dragases, to Mohammed, *that you desire war more than peace, since I cannot satisfy you either by my protestations of sincerity, or by my readiness to swear allegiance, so let it be according to your desire. I turn now and look to God alone. Should it be his will that the city be yours, where is*

Illustration opposite: Portrait of the Sultan Mohammed II, probably painted by Giovanni Bellini, in the National Gallery, London.

127

he who can oppose it? If he should inspire you with a desire for peace, I shall be only too happy. However, I release you from all your oaths and treaties with me, and, closing the gates of my capital, I will defend my people to the last drop of my blood. Reign in happiness until the All-Just, the Supreme God, calls us both before his judgement seat. [70] Preparations for the siege had been in progress since the end of the previous year; already Mohammed's monster cannon were drawn up into position, and the rest of his army—estimated at anything between seventy thousand and a hundred and forty thousand fighting men—had been marshalled under the city's walls. On 6 April the Sultan and his suite arrived, and on 11 April the Turkish cannonade began.

For the following six weeks the siege continued, resisted from within by the Emperor at the head of but some seven thousand fighting men. Among these latter were some two thousand foreign troops that included a detachment of five hundred Genoese under the command, *per benefitio de la Christianitade et per honor de lo mundo*, of Juan Giustiniani di Longo. This detachment held the crucial St. Romanus Gate opposite which the Turks had placed their heaviest cannon and best soldiers and opposite which, too, the Sultan, surrounded by his white-capped Janissaries, had taken up his stand. At the beginning of May the Emperor was urged by the senators and the Patriarch to leave, and Giustiniani, himself in favour of the plan, placed his ships at the Emperor's disposal. *The Emperor listened to all this quietly and patiently. At last, after having been for some time deep in thought, he began to speak: 'I thank you all for the advice which you have given me. I know that my going out of the city might be of some benefit to me, inasmuch as all that you foresee might really happen. But it is impossible for me to go away: how could I leave the churches of our Lord, and His servants the clergy, and the throne, and my people in such a plight? What would the world say of me? I pray you, my friends, in future do not say to me anything else but, "Nay, sire, do not leave us." Never, never will I leave you. I am resolved to die here with you.' And saying this, the Emperor turned his head aside, because tears filled his eyes; and with him wept the Patriarch and all who were there.* [71]

On 23 May the final offer of the Turkish envoy to the Emperor, of a kingdom in the Peloponnese and a free passage to all citizens, was rejected, although by now the desperateness of the position—the lack of men to continue the defence of the fourteen miles of wall, the failure of any relief to arrive from the West, the absence of supernatural intervention—would have given good grounds for surrender. But still the Turks were hesitant: should they call the siege off? They decided to try one final assault and if that failed to abandon the city. On the evening of 28 May Mohammed made the round of his troops; he spoke to them of the city they were to take, of the treasures in its palaces and private houses, its churches with silver and gold and precious stones, of girls young and lovely, boys of good stock, houses and beautiful gardens. Those who died fighting for the faith would enter directly into Paradise. Those who lived would be given leave to pillage the city for three days: 'All its wealth, its silver, gold, silk, cloth and women, will be yours; only the buildings and the walls will be reserved for the Sultan.' And as he finished, from the ranks of his soldiery rose the repeated cry, '*Lâ ilaha ill-Allâh, Mohammed ressoul-Allâh*' (There is no God but God, and Mohammed is his Prophet).

Meanwhile, the besieged inside the city had learnt of the Sultan's decision and the pending attack. On that same Monday afternoon a solemn procession moved through the streets and squares of Constantinople. All, Orthodox and Latins, bishops and priests, monks and nuns, laymen and women, the city's children, took part in it, bearing with them the miraculous icons, the bones of saints, golden and jewelled crosses. At each shrine, at each weak point in the walls, the procession halted, the priests read prayers, the bishops raised their croziers and blessed the soldiers, sprinkling them with holy water from bunches of dry basil. Towards sundown, before Vespers, the Emperor gathered round him the commanders of the troops and the chief citizens, Greek and foreign. He spoke to them: 'Brothers and fellow-citizens, be ready for the morn. If God gives us grace and valour, and the Holy Trinity help us, in whom alone we trust, we will do such deeds that the foe shall fall back in shame before our arms.' He turned to the Genoese, to the Venetians, to address them separately: '"I pray you now show us in this difficult hour that you are indeed our companions, our faithful allies, and our brethren."... Then the wretched Romans strengthened their hearts like lions, sought and gave pardon, and with tears embraced each other as though mindful no more of wife or children or earthly goods, but only of death... which they were glad to undergo.' And they repaired to the great church of St. Sophia, 'to strengthen themselves by prayer and the reception of the Holy Mysteries, to confirm their vows to fight, and, if need be, mindless of all worldly interests, to die for the honour of God and Christianity'.[72]

The Emperor entered the already full church. Once more, and only once more, the marble walls, the mosaic vaults, the ambo and iconostasis, the hangings, the plate, the lamps, the vestments served in a Christian ritual. Patriarch and Cardinal, with a crowd of ecclesiastics both Orthodox and Roman; Emperor and nobles, all that was left of the once proud and splendid Byzantine aristocracy; soldiers and citizens, Constantinopolitans, Venetians, Genoese: all were present, all conscious that at last the 'final hour' was upon them. The Emperor prayed with great fervour. Leaving the imperial seat and approaching the iconostasis, he prostrated himself before the icons of Christ and Our Lady, sought pardon from every prelate for any wrong that he might ever have done to any of them, embraced each of them, and then went to the altar to partake of the 'undefiled and divine mysteries'. In the sight of his priests, his soldiers, his people, he prepared, in this liturgy of death, to appear before his God. As the last Christian Emperor of Constantinople turned and left the shrine where for so many centuries his predecessors and people had worshipped, the great congregation wept aloud.

Back at his Palace, the Emperor, in the manner of kings, asked pardon from his dependents for any harshness or injustice he might have shown them. 'Had a man been made of wood or stone he must have wept', wrote the chronicler later.[73] Then all returned to their posts, and stationing themselves between the outer wall and the inner wall, locked the doors of the latter behind them so that any retreat was impossible. Late in the evening Constantine himself left the Palace, mounted his Arabian horse, and with his suite rode towards the walls for his final tour of inspection. The night was dark and sultry; large drops of water fell, then stopped; the muffled sound of the Turks preparing ladders by the moat came through the obscurity. Before cock-crow the Emperor had taken up his post near the St. Romanus Gate. Thus, 'each side having prayed to its God, we to ours and they to theirs, the Lord Almighty with His Mother in heaven decided that they must be avenged in this battle of the morrow for all the sins committed'.[74]

At the first streak of dawn on 29 May the assault began. Again and again the Turks attacked, to the sound of cymbals and flutes, the metallic ring of weapons, the boom of cannon, the tremor of resounding shot; again and again they were forced back, only to meet and to be pressed forward again by the on-coming waves of the troops behind. Then at the critical moment a deep wound forced Giustiniani to retire from his key post in the defences. Noticing the confusion at this vital spot, Mohammed ordered the Janissaries to attack. One of them, a gigantic man, Hassan Ulubadli, holding his shield in his left hand, fought his way against showers of stones and arrows up the ladder to the top of the wall, followed by some thirty others. He was overpowered and killed, but his companions broke through, climbed the top of the wall, and were in the city. 'The city is taken', rose the cry, as other Turkish troops forced their way past the heaps of dead and dying into the streets of Constantinople and Turkish banners began to appear on the turrets of some of the towers. 'The city is taken and I am still alive'—such are the last recorded words of the Emperor Constantine Palaeologus Dragases as, dismounting from his horse, casting from him the insignia of his office, he plunged into and disappeared for ever amid the final charge of the Janissaries.

By eight o'clock in the morning the city was in Turkish hands and the three-day promised sack had begun. There is no need to speak of the slaughter and the pillage, except to say that, frightful as they were, they were less frightful than those of the Christian crusaders of 1204. Towards noon (or, according to some, the following day) the Conqueror, accompanied by his Viziers, Pashas, and Ulemas, and escorted by his bodyguard of Janissaries, entered the city. He rode straight to the church of St. Sophia. Dismounting, he stooped down at the threshold, scooped up a handful of earth, and let it fall on his turbaned head as an act of humiliation before the God who had given him victory. He then entered the church and ordered one of his Court-Ulemas to ascend the pulpit and to deliver a prayer, while he himself mounted what had been the Christian altar and there made his first *Rika'at* in his new capital. Thus did the great church dedicated to the Immortal Wisdom of Christ, heart of the Christian city of Constantinople and symbol of its deepest hope and promise, change into the mosque Aya-Sofia of the Moslem Stamboul; and, as the most famous of Ottoman historians, Sa'd-ud-din, was to write a century or so later, *that wide region, that strong and lofty city, from being the land of hostility* (dār-ul-harb), *became the city where money is coined* (dār-uz-zarb); *and from being the nest of the owl of errors, was turned into the capital of glory and honour. Through the noble efforts of the Mohammedan Sultan, for the evil-voiced clash of the bells of the shameless misbelievers was substituted the Moslem call to prayer, the sweet five-times-repeated chant of the Paracletic Faith of the glorious rites; and the ears of the people of the Djihâd were filled with the melody of the ezan. The churches which were within the city were emptied of their vile idols, and cleansed from their filthy and idolatrous impurities; and by the defacement of their images, and the erection of the Islami* mihrabs *and pulpits, many monasteries and chapels became the envy of the Gardens of Paradise. The temples of the misbelievers were turned into the mosques of the pious, and the rays of the light of Islam drove away the hosts of darkness from the place so long the abode of the despicable infidels, and the streaks of the dawn of the Faith dispelled the lurid darkness of oppression, for the word, irresistible as destiny, of the fortunate sultan became supreme in the governance of this new dominion.... On the first Friday* (after the capture) *prayers were recited in Aya-Sofia, and in the sultan's glorious name was the Mohammedan* Khutba (Friday prayer containing the name of the sovereign) *read. Thus, that ancient edifice was illumined with the rays of the Orthodox Faith, and perfumed with the breath of the odours of the Noble Law; and as the hearts of the* Muvahhidin (those who testify to the Unity of God) *were filled with joy at the erection of the emblems of the Faith, so that most desirable of shrines, that lofty mosque, that heart-pleasing temple, was full of the people of Islam; and its delight-reflecting interior, by being burnished with the Declaration of the Unity, became brilliant as a polished mirror.*[75]

Illustration opposite: One of the last Byzantine Emperors, Manuel II Palaeologus. Miniature from a MS. of the funeral prayer spoken by the Emperor Manuel on the death of his brother Theodore, Despot of the Morea, in 1407. Bibliothèque Nationale, Paris.

κ ω σε παντα ρί σε πε υν θη σω ν ο μω σ,
βλε πω μα ι δα κρύ ω, ου θε πω δ ρο σω τα φ·
σ ε σ αυ του ελε γε κ ρα πι στ μι κ μ α του
ο σ ου χ ρε ι α σ α ζα σ θα ι, ω σ δ οι ο πε μ οι
ου π ω σα ι π α σ α ι δ σω η λθο ν ε σα μα,

Ει και προσ αυ του τον ξη πα ν πα ω ε κα
η μα σ δ ε αυ τοι σ και π ρο σου φι λ πα τε μοι·
αλλα και κο σμ η σω σε πα ι σ α φ η μι α ι σ
τ ο γαρ κα τα ξ ι α ν ου ρο τω π ν ρο σ·
σ ω δ α ζ γ ε κα ν ο ι μ α ι δ μ α ν ρα ν ο λω σ:·

[κ ω πε μ η θη σω μ   .ω ν
κ αι σε λε μ π α ν
α ρι ζε, α και π ρο σ
δ ν εκ δ ε λ ν ικ κ   α σ
η φ ι σι γαρ, ου δ ι
δ α σι να δ α κρ υ π
τα ρ τα φ ον θε α σ
θα ι. η μα σ δ αυ το
και π ρο σου, οι ο
τ ρ κ ρα τι στ ου σ ω ν
α ρ μ εν α φ κ ρη
κ α σ α υ του δ ε ον
δ ε ου κ αι τ οι σ πα ι
νο ι σ κ ο σμ η σ α ι σ ε
τ ρ χ ρ ε ι σ α δ φ ο σι
ω σ ε λ λ α τ ο γαρ
κα τ α ξ ί α ν, ου δ α ν
ου δ α π α σ μ ε δ ν
θ ρ ω π η φ ο σ ε ν ο γ ο
π α σ α ι δ α π α σ α ι
ι σ. α υ του λ α κ ρι β
σ ω η κ η λ θο ν, σ ω φ α
δ η ε ι κα ν ο λω σ
θ η ρ η:·

Ι C Ν Ο
Ν Α Ε Μ
Χ Ω Δ Ω
Λ Ω Σ Β Α
C Ι Λ ι

 Κ ΑΙ ΤΟ
Κ Α Ν Τ Ο Ρ
ΡΩ Μ Α Ι Ο
C Π Α Λ ε
Ο Λ Ο ΓΟ

Illustration opposite: View up into the dome of St. Sophia, showing an Islamic inscription in place of the former picture of Christ Pantocrator.

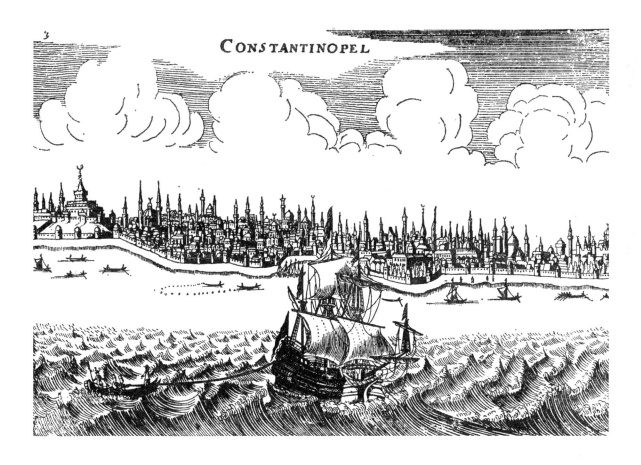

Turkish Constantinople: Istanbul. Woodcut of the seventeenth century.

REFERENCES

1 Procopius, *Buildings*, I. v. 11–13.

2 For this and other references to and quotations concerning the consecration and dedication of Constantinople, see *Scriptores originum Constantinopolitanarum*, ed. T. Preger (Leipzig, 1901), passim, but esp. Πάτρια Κωνσταντινοπόλεως. See also D. Lathoud, 'La Consécration et la dédicace de Constantinople', in *Echos d'Orient* XXII (1924) et seq.

3 Fulk of Chartres.

4 *The Book of the Prefect*. English translation by E. H. Freshfield, *Roman Law in the Later Roman Empire* (Cambridge, 1938).

5 Ibid.

6 See *The Conquest of Constantinople*, trans. from the old French of Robert of Clari by E. H. McNeal (Columbia University Press), p. 101.

7 See Geoffroi de Villehardouin, *Conquête de Constantinople*, trans. into modern French by M. Natalis de Wailly (Paris, 1882), p. 73.

8 Procopius, op. cit., I. ii. 1–12.

9 Procopius, op. cit., I. x. 11–20.

10 See Constantinus Porphyrogenitus, *De ceremoniis aulae bizantinae*, ed. J. J. Reiske and I. Bekker (Corpus Scriptorum Historiae Byzantinae, Bonn, 1829–40), Vol. I, p. 569.

11 See Theophanes Continuatus, *Historia*, ed. I. Bekker (Corpus Scriptorum Historiae Byzantinae, Bonn, 1839), pp. 332–5.

12 From the *Chronicon Paschale*, ed. L. Dindorf (Corpus Scriptorum Historiae Byzantinae, Bonn, 1832), 2 vols., cited by W. R. Lethaby and H. Swainson, *The Church of Sancta Sophia Constantinople* (London, 1894), p. 15.

13 Procopius, op. cit., I. i. 20–25.

14 This and other translations from Paul the Silentiary's poem are from Lethaby and Swainson, op. cit.

15 From 'A Twelfth-Century Description of St. Sophia', trans. by C. Mango and J. Parker in *Dumbarton Oaks Papers* No. 14 (1960), pp. 233 ff.

16 Procopius, op. cit., I. i. 46.

17 Paul the Silentiary.

18 Ibid.

19 Procopius, op. cit., I. i. 61–65.

20 The two works on St. Sophia of which I have made most use are (1) the monograph already cited, by Lethaby and Swainson; and (2) *Hagia Sophia*, by E. H. Swift (Columbia, 1940).

21 Philotheus, Patriarch of Constantinople (mid-fourteenth century), cited by J. Meyendorff, *L'Iconographie de la Sagesse Divine*, Cahiers archéologiques, Vol. X, p. 262.

22 Epistle to the Romans, 13. 1–5.

23 See D. S. Wallace-Hadrill, *Eusebius of Caesarea* (London, 1960), pp. 169–71.

24 Eusebius, *Panegyricus*, 2.

25 Eusebius, *De Vita Constantini*, Bk. IV, ch. xxiv.

26 From 'Le Pèlerinage d'Ignace de Smolensk' (1389 to 1405) in *Itinéraires russes en Orient*, trans. for the Société de l'Orient Latin by Mme. B. de Khitrowo (Geneva, 1889), pp. 143 ff., amended from the Russian sixteenth-century *Nikon Chronicle* (*Complete Collection of Russian Chronicles*, Vol. XI, pp. 101–4) by Dimitri Obolensky.

27 See R. Guilland, 'Le Droit divin à Byzance', in his *Etudes byzantines* (Paris, 1959), pp. 207 ff.

28 From *The Works of Liudprand of Cremona*, trans. by F. A. Wright (London, 1930), pp. 207–8.

29 Ibid. pp. 209 ff.

30 Ibid.

31 Procopius, *The Anecdota* or *Secret History*, XV. 12–16.

32 Procopius, *History of the Wars*, I. xxiv. 32–37.

33 Michael Psellus, *Chronographia*, Book VI, trans. by E. R. A. Sewter, *The Chronographia of Michael Psellus* (London, 1953), p. 137.

34 Ibid., p. 138.

35 Anna Comnena, *The Alexiad*, trans. by E. A. S. Dawes, *The Alexiad of Anna Comnena* (London, 1928), p. 135.

36 From 'The Travels of Bertrandon de la Brocquière, A.D. 1432 and 1433', in *Early Travels in Palestine*, ed. Thomas Wright (London, 1848), pp. 338–9.

37 See G. Schlumberger, *Un Empereur byzantin au dixième siècle: Nicéphore Phocas* (Paris, 1890), pp. 67 ff., on which this account is based.

38 By A. Rambaud, in *Etudes sur l'histoire byzantine* (Paris, 1912). It is on his essay on the Hippodrome that the description which follows is based.

39 Gospel according to St. John, 18. 36.

40 From 'Harun-Ibn-Yahya and his description of Constantinople' by A. Vasiliev, in *Seminarium Kondakovianum*, V (Prague, 1932).

41 From 'The Russian Primary Chronicle', trans. by S. H. Cross, *Harvard Studies and Notes in Philology and Literature*, v. XII (Cambridge, Mass., 1930).

42 The Revelation of St. John, 21. 2–3.

43 From Homily IX of *Homilies of Photius*, trans. by C. Mango (Harvard University Press, 1958).

44 The Revelation of St. John, 21. 18–24.

45 F. Combefis, *Historia Haeresis Monothelitarum* (Paris, 1648), col. 754.

46 See N. H. Baynes, *Byzantine Studies and Other Essays* (London, 1955), pp. 240 ff., for a full account of the finding of this robe.

47 For St. Andrew the Fool for Christ (St. Andrew Salus) and the Virgin of Blachernae, see *Acta Sanctorum Boll.*, 28 May, VI, pp. 1–112 (= Migne, *P. G.*, III, 627–88).

48 First verse of the Akathistos Hymn. See, for origin of and other details concerning this hymn, E. Wellesz, 'The "Akathistos". A Study in Byzantine Hymnography', in *Dumbarton Oaks Papers* Nos. 9 and 10 (1956), pp. 141 ff.

49 From Homily IV of *Homilies of Photius*, op. cit.

50 See Cananus, *De Constantinopoli Oppugnata*, ed. I. Bekker (Corpus Scriptorum Historiae Byzantinae, Bonn, 1838), pp. 457 ff.

51 From the Oration, *In S. Mariae Zonam*, by Archbishop Germanos, Patriarch of Constantinople (715 to 730), Migne, *P. G.*, LXXXXVIII, 372–84.

52 From *Itinéraires russes en Orient*, op. cit.; English trans. by Lethaby and Swainson in *The Church of Sancta Sophia*, op. cit., pp. 101 ff.

53 Leo Sternbach, 'Analecta Avarica', in the *Rozprawy* of the Academy of Cracow (1900), p. 304. Cited by Baynes, op. cit., p. 249.

54 From 'To my Pupil Nicolas', trans. by A. Gardner, *Theodore of Studium* (London, 1905), pp. 71 ff.

55 From Discourse XXVII, trans. by Gardner, op. cit., pp. 91 ff.

56 From *Vie de Syméon le nouveau théologien (949–1022)* par Nicétas Stéthatos. Texte grec inédit, ed. etc. par Le P. Irénée Hausherr S. I. (*Orientalia Christiana*, Vol. XII, No. 45, Rome 1928), II, 11–12, pp. 18–19.

57 From *Three Byzantine Saints*, Contemporary Biographies translated from the Greek by E. Dawes and N. H. Baynes (Oxford, 1948), pp. 7 ff.

58 2nd Prooemium to the Akathistos Hymn.

59 St. Paul's Epistle to the Galatians, 4. 26.

60 See on this subject Ch. Diehl, 'De quelques croyances byzantines sur la fin de Constantinople', in *Byz.*

Zeitschrift, XXX (1929–30), pp. 192 ff.; and A. Vasiliev, 'Medieval Ideas of the End of the World: East and West', in *Byzantion* XVI (1942–43), pp. 462 ff.

61 Cited by Vasiliev, loc. cit.

62 See 'A Letter of the Patriarch Antonius to Vasili I, Grand Prince of Russia', in E. Barker, *Social and Political Thought in Byzantium* (Oxford, 1957), pp. 194 ff.

63 See *The Conquest of Constantinople*, from the old French of Robert of Clari, op. cit., pp. 110 ff.

64 From Homily III of *Homilies of Photius*, op. cit.

65 Cited by L. Oeconomos, in 'L'Etat intellectuel et moral des Byzantins au XIVᵉ siècle', *Mélanges Charles Diehl*, Vol. I (Paris, 1932), pp. 225 ff. See also on this theme: I. Ševčenko, 'The Decline of Byzantium seen through the Eyes of its Intellectuals', in *Dumbarton Oaks Papers*, No. 15 (1961), pp. 167 ff.

66 See G. Butler, *Anna Comnena* (Oxford, 1929), pp. 438 ff.

67 See Geoffroi de Villehardouin, *Conquête de Constantinople*, op. cit., p. 131.

68 S. Runciman, *A History of the Crusades*, Vol. III (Cambridge, 1954), pp. 123–4.

69 See L. Massignon, 'Le Mirage byzantin dans le miroir bagdadien d'il y a mille ans', in *Mélanges Henri Grégoire*, 2 (Bruxelles, 1950), pp. 428 ff., to which these notes are indebted.

70 Michael Ducas, *Historia Byzantina*, ed. I. Bekker (Corpus Scriptorum Historiae Byzantinae, Bonn, 1834), p. 245.

71 Cited by M. Chedomil Mijatovich, *Constantine the Last Emperor of the Greeks* (London, 1892), pp. 173–4, from the Slavonic Chronicle, *The Reports of the Capture of Constantinople by the Godless Turkish Sultan*.

72 George Phrantzes, *Annales*, ed. I. Bekker (Corpus Scriptorum Historiae Byzantinae, Bonn, 1839), pp. 271 ff.

73 Phrantzes, loc. cit.

74 Nicolò Barbaro, *Giornale dell'assedio di Constantinopoli*, ed. E. Cornet (Vienna, 1856), cited by E. Pears, *The Destruction of the Greek Empire* (London, 1903), p. 332.

75 From *The Capture of Constantinople from the Taj-ut-Tevarikh, of Khoja Sa'd-ud-Din*, trans. by E. J. W. Gibb (Glasgow, 1874).

Extracts from the undermentioned sources are included by kind permission of the publishers and others concerned:

28 Messrs. Routledge & Kegan Paul Ltd.

43 Dumbarton Oaks Trustees for Harvard University.

54 Messrs. Edward Arnold (Publishers) Ltd.

57 Messrs. Blackwell & Mott Ltd.

65 Presses Universitaires de France.

The map on page 6 is reproduced by permission of Oklahoma University Press, with the concurrence of Messrs. Macmillan & Co. Ltd.

LIST OF ILLUSTRATIONS

(Those marked * are in colour)